PRAISE FOR *BE A FREE RANGE HUMAN*

'A practical guidebook loaded with exactly the tools you need to break free of excuses and start creating the adventurous life of your dreams. Marianne Cantwell knows what she's talking about. Pay attention.'
Barbara Winter, author of *Making A Living Without A Job*

'There isn't just *one* way to create a life and business that fits who you are in our fast-changing world. Read this if you want to awaken new possibilities and find the path that's right for you.'
Dorie Clark, author of *Reinventing You* and *Entrepreneurial You* and Faculty, Duke University's Fuqua School of Business

'*Be a Free Range Human* shines. Marianne Cantwell could have merely inspired millions of frustrated cubicle-dwellers to think outside the job box, but she goes the extra mile to provide the reader with the all-important "how". Brilliant!'
Dr Valerie Young, author *The Secret Thoughts of Successful Women* and guest speaker at universities including Stanford, Princeton, Oxford and Harvard

'Imaginative, inspirational, and challenging. A unique, well written book that will have a huge impact on readers.'
Dr Barrie Hopson, author of 40 books including *Build Your Own Rainbow* and *And What Do You Do? 10 Steps to Creating a Portfolio Career*

'Pragmatic, practical and inspirational – a grounded call to action to build a career, and more importantly a life, that works for us as individuals. I would give this to anyone who is feeling stuck or who feels that there is more to life than how they are currently living. There is not one identikit route that we all need to take in order to be successful or happy. This book will help you find your own way.'
Marianne Power, author of the international bestseller
Help Me! How Self-Help Has Not Changed My Life

'A rare mix of funny, frank and feisty, as well as realistic and do-able, this is the kind of book you'll take everywhere with you – it'll be your new best buddy, supporting and encouraging you on the road to living la vida free range-a!'
Nadia Finer, author of *Little Me Big Business* **and co-author of** *More To Life Than Shoes*

'Being "free range" is no longer a niche, quirky trend. With an abundance of tools and opportunities, creating a career and life on your terms is now a mainstream option. In a world that can feel like its teetering on the edge, the ones seizing the moment in a period of disruption are designing work and lifestyles that allow them to quickly adapt and be more creative. There are some wonderful guides to help us get out and thrive, and none better than Marianne Cantwell's.'
Ben Keene, co-founder of Tribe Wanted, co-founder of the Rebel Book Club and former startup leader at Escape The City

'I love Marianne's advice, I love this book – a fantastic mix of inspiring and practical. This second edition has really taken it to another level. Reading *Be A Free Range Human* is like sitting down in a coffee shop and having a 1 to 1 with someone who knows what she's talking about, and who actually cares that you live a life that's meaningful. Read this and Marianne will not only help you dream bigger, she'll also show you the little steps you can take today to get there.'
James Wallman, bestselling author of *Stuffocation: Living More with Less* **and** *Time And How To Spend It*

'When I read *Be A Free Range Human*, it felt as though a million lightbulbs went off at once; I had an idea of what I wanted but I didn't think it could be done without compromising my own mental health and introverted nature. This book changed my perspective. Today, I've published two books, and The Blurt Foundation has reached and educated hundreds of thousands of people (with over a million unique users on our website). This book gave me the confidence to craft a life that suits my personality and personal situation. I still dip into it today.'
Jayne Hardy, author of *The Self-Care Project* and founder of The Blurt Foundation

'Do you find yourself wishing for a better life, to see more, to do things that light you up – and to earn a good living doing so? Read this book. *Be A Free Range Human* was *the* catalyst for the changes in my life which took me from feeling like life was passing me by, to place to where I am now with a life, businesses (and freedom) I never thought I'd have. Today hundreds of thousands people come to my work, and many ask for advice about how to change things and get going – and all I can say is, this is the book that started me on the journey. I cannot recommend reading this enough.'
Dan Meredith, author the international bestseller *How To Be F*cking Awesome*

COMHAIRLE CHONTAE ÁTHA CLIATH THEAS
SOUTH DUBLIN COUNTY LIBRARIES
BALLYROAN BRANCH LIBRARY
TO RENEW ANY ITEM TEL: 494 1900
OR ONLINE AT www.southdublinlibraries.ie

Items should be returned on or before the last date below. Fines, as displayed in the Library, will be charged on overdue items.

First published in Great Britain and the United States in 2013 by Kogan Page Limited
Second edition published in 2019

Apart from any fair dealing for the purposes of research or private study, or criticism or review, as permitted under the Copyright, Designs and Patents Act 1988, this publication may only be reproduced, stored or transmitted, in any form or by any means, with the prior permission in writing of the publishers, or in the case of reprographic reproduction in accordance with the terms and licences issued by the CLA. Enquiries concerning reproduction outside these terms should be sent to the publishers at the undermentioned addresses:

2nd Floor, 45 Gee Street
London
EC1V 3RS
United Kingdom
www.koganpage.com

122 W 27th St, 10th Floor
New York, NY 10001
USA

4737/23 Ansari Road
Daryaganj
New Delhi 110002
India

© Marianne Cantwell, 2013, 2019

The right of Marianne Cantwell to be identified as the author of this work has been asserted by her in accordance with the Copyright, Designs and Patents Act 1988.

ISBNs
Hardback   978 1 78966 016 6
Paperback   978 0 7494 9709 5
Ebook   978 0 7494 9710 1

British Library Cataloguing-in-Publication Data

A CIP record for this book is available from the British Library.

Library of Congress Cataloging-in-Publication Data

Names: Cantwell, Marianne, author.
Title: Be a free range human : escape the 9-5, create a life you love and still pay the bills / Marianne Cantwell.
Description: Second edition. | London ; New York, NY : Kogan Page, 2019. | Includes bibliographical references and index. |
Identifiers: LCCN 2019022774 (print) | LCCN 2019022775 (ebook) | ISBN 9780749487805 (hardback) | ISBN 9780749482978 (paperback) | ISBN 9780749482985 (ebook)
Subjects: LCSH: Career development. | Job satisfaction. | Self-employed. | Flextime.
Classification: LCC HF5381 .C26155 2019 (print) | LCC HF5381 (ebook) | DDC 650.1–dc23
LC record available at https://lccn.loc.gov/2019022774
LC ebook record available at https://lccn.loc.gov/2019022775

Typeset by Hong Kong FIVE Workshop
Print production managed by Jellyfish
Printed and bound by CPI Group (UK) Ltd, Croydon, CR0 4YY

Life can be much broader once you discover one simple fact: everything around you that you call life was made up by people that were no smarter than you. And you can change it, you can influence it, you can build your own things...

The minute that you understand that you can poke life, you can mould it... once you learn that, you'll never be the same again.

Steve Jobs

CONTENTS

PART THREE Think like a free range human 87

You don't need a wildly original idea, oodles of experience, or even funding. How to start with what you have (and find out if your idea will work in two weeks). Decide on your new free range career (and make it fit you).

PART FOUR Build your free range escape
hatch 173

Get started, stand out from the crowd, get known
fast and get paid (without changing your personality).
How to make things work and break free, on your terms.

PREFACE TO THE SECOND EDITION

In the past the problem was that we didn't have enough information. Today we're bombarded with it. Yet clarity seems harder to come by than ever, doesn't it? So the question is:

In a world of noise, how do you hear clearly enough to know what is truly the right next step for you?

That's exactly where this book slides into your life.

When the first edition of this book came out in 2013, the world was a different place: fake news wasn't a thing (but Twitter really was), the financial crash of 2008 was fresh in people's minds – and more to the point the conversation about making a move to *doing something you love* and *making a living without a boss* felt very different.

There wasn't a newsfeed full of perfect shiny comparisons a click away.

There weren't '5 step blueprints for freedom' at every scroll.

Instead it was a creative, playful space that gave a damn about who you were. But not long after the book came out, something shifted.

I watched a swathe of 'formulas' and 'systems for success' sweep the internet that led to people going from squishing themselves into one box in order to get paid... only to find themselves in another box of someone else's making.

'Create life and income on your terms' suddenly seemed to mean 'Follow these steps to become a carbon copy of this person!'

This wasn't freedom.

More to the point it led to too many people hitting a wall. Because that copycat approach *rarely works in practice for people like us* (you'll discover why in this book, and what works better).

I felt like I was suddenly at the centre of (and one of the accidental founders of) a scene that I would never have chosen to be a part of in that form.

So I did something I never expected – I stepped away.

I loved what I did but the environment was no longer my home – and I stepped back to figure things out.

I took some time offline and even shut down some online products that people loved, because they felt too similar to a movement I no longer wanted to be in (yes, this was hard, but it felt right).

Instead I spent time, well… painting, writing for me, exploring, doing projects, developing fresh ideas and testing them with real people – some of which led to some key updates in this book! – as well as personal things like buying and renovating my first property (and, *yes*, luckily the business I had created let me do that!).

Out of that time came some things I didn't expect: firstly, a TEDx Talk, *The Hidden Power Of Not (Always) Fitting In*, which went a bit viral and led to fresh opportunities; a move to a new country; but most surprisingly of all, at the end of it… *a fire in my belly.*

To step back in and bring *'create life on your terms'* back to what it says on the tin. You see:

> *The idea of changing up your life and doing something as you was* never *about creating something that looked impressive to anonymous strangers on the internet or to the committee of critics in your head –* it was about getting real to create something that feels good to you. *Something that really works for you. In reality, not just on paper.*
>
> *This edition is bringing that back even more.*

(That was always what this book was about – and now it does so even more strongly.)

This book been translated around the world; we have emails every week from people who read it and made a change because of it – and it's time to update it to cut through the noise of today's world to what matters for you, here and now.

So: have you ever felt that no solution fully fits you? Or have a secret sense that you'll have to leave a piece of yourself at the door in order to get paid? You're in the right place. I'll show you how to use free range thinking to create a solution that is tailor made to fit you (and what you want).

For those who have read the first edition, a few of my favourite changes to look out for are:

'The Three Free Range Styles' (Chapter 24). Go beyond 'one size fits all' formulas and discover how to make things work for who you are. In Part 4, this new chapter reveals how three different *'free range' personality styles* bring in clients and income. *Note: this replaces the old chapter on creating a following and an email list – that is still available as a bonus download within the new chapter but is no longer the only way.*

'But What If I'm Not A Shiny-Haired, Always-Confident Entrepreneur?' (Chapter 17). Here we go under the surface of glossy success stories (including sharing a part of my story I didn't share in the first edition).

'Overcoming Information Overwhelm' (Chapter 31). Two 'filters' you can use to cut through the piles of information (and 'should dos') out there, to focus on the best next steps for *you*.

Tweaks, upgrades (and new additions!) throughout to bring this to life even more.

What you're about to read is not a book about being a 'rebel', nor is it a book about hopping on the latest bandwagon because that's what the cool kids are doing (or because that's what some shouty guru in the videos is saying you 'must' do in order to be good enough).

It's a book about grounded, smart thinking about what matters here and now: *creating a life and income on your terms that suits the person you are in every way.*

Because that is, and always has been, more than enough.

So let's get started.

Marianne x

ACKNOWLEDGEMENTS

Rebecca Bush. Without you this second edition wouldn't exist. Thank you and the team for believing in this book (and for your integrity in bringing me back to the publishing world in such a thoughtful way).

Selina Barker. The other half of my free range mind, my longest collaborator, and one of the best humans I know. As always, this book has your touch all over it.

Nicole Est and Jeanne Patti. I can't thank you enough for your time and input throughout this revision. Watching you own your 'super-powers', and help others as a result, makes me very happy. Looking forward to our free range adventures ahead!

Marianne Power for reading the updates and offering your wise edits and support, **Barbara Winter** for being at the end of the phone when needed (and **Monica Srivastava** for calmly holding the fort on emails and more while I disappeared into my creating cave). Thank you for your time and kindness.

Friends who were so supportive (even when I could 'only talk about the book' for months at a time), including those who helped with all my 'international questions' (looking at you Helen, Catherine, Jess, Kim, Lisa, Dave, Osmaan, Sarah, Steve, Michael C, Emily, Andrew, James… the list is too long to fit here but I am grateful for every one!).

To my Dad, for going from utterly unsure of what your daughter does for a living (or why she threw away several 'good careers'), to one of my biggest supporters today. How you have taken to the free range ideas over the years has made me happier than almost anything else.

To **Michael.** aka 'other M'. Your fierce love and support to the finish line and beyond means everything.

To **free range test readers.** From guinea-pigging the exercises to giving feedback, you grounded this book and made sure every page works for real.

To **the free range tribe (readers and online).** From reading and responding to messages, taking part in events/courses, to spreading the free range ideas in your own ways – everything that has happened with this book is because of you. I hope this edition hits home even more!

And most of all to you, who picked up this book. Welcome in.

This one's for you.

PROLOGUE

Alarm rings. Get up. Feed cat. Late to work. Walk up the hill and down into the tube station. This is all I'll see of the outside world all day.

Every morning the same commute, packed in a train so closely that all I can see and smell is the next person's armpit.

Standing there I look at the people around me. We are supposed to be some of the most successful humans of our generation and we are sleep deprived, stressed and packed into a metal box on our way to an office-shaped box. Someone isn't wearing deodorant. The guy next to me, in the Hugo Boss suit, is listening to dance music on his phone, pretending to be alive for just one moment.

The doors open and more people cram in so that every part of my body is touching someone else's. I can't breathe.

Someone steps on my foot and I can't move out of the way. If we were animals this would not be legal. Battery cage humans going from our commute cage to our career cage, when all I want to do is run out of there, past the buildings and roam free in the sunshine. The thought strikes me, 'I want to be a free range human'.

Then someone's elbow strikes me and I forget all about that crazy dream.

For now.

Introduction

From beach to boardroom

'Enjoy your adventures now,' said my Dad, 'you won't be able to do that sort of thing when you...'

And just then the line went. I was on a payphone – remember those? – in Koh Samui. I was 22. Feet in the sand, flip-flops in my hand and a queue of bedraggled Full Moon backpackers outside, waiting to make their calls. This was the first time I'd talked to Dad for a month, and I'd just told him I was going trekking in the jungle.

'Can't hear you, Dad...'

'I said...' he shouted through the bad line '... you won't be able to do that sort of thing when you grow up and get a proper job.'

Did anyone ever tell you the same thing? After all, that's how life is supposed to be, isn't it? Have fun, then settle down, commute, work, commute, die (with a few years at the end, if you're lucky).

Dreams aren't meant to last. They're what you have when you're young and foolish. They're what you give up when you get a real job. *Everyone knows that.*

Everyone except, it seemed, the 22-year-old me. Standing in the sunshine, phone in hand, I just laughed. Why would I do that? This was wonderful. I couldn't see anything that would make me give up this life of freedom!

Fast-forward a few years later and I was firmly seconded in a corporate job. Sitting at my desk, I adjusted my Prada glasses,

The mission? Freedom and fulfilment: not in retirement, not in their annual vacation, but every single day, starting now. These people are the new Free Range Humans.

Free Range Humans work when, where and how they want and get paid to do what they love. Today you can find Free Range Humans all around the world working happily with their laptops from parks, cafés, beaches and their kitchen tables, making a great living without an office or a boss:

- Some free rangers use their new-found independence to travel the world full-time, such as Hannah and Chris, who left office life to help companies hire better talent... while on their laptops on the other side of the world.

- Others stay at home and spend time with their families, such as Emma, who left her job as a marketing campaign manager to make a full-time living from YouTube videos... and watch her kids grow up.

- Others take the opportunity to pack everything they love into a portfolio career so that they don't have to settle on choosing just one thing, such as Carla, who quit her job in the city and now is a photographer and also runs a stationery subscription service.

- Others use the free range approach to break into their dream field without having to convince an employer to hire them as a career changer, such as Charlie, who went from regular office bod to running amazing urban writers' retreats.

- And, of course, others create a life that allows them to make an income while offline, unplugged and lying in a hammock with a mojito (that would be me – on some days!).

The free range tribe isn't united by travel or a particular industry: this growing tribe is united in taking a unique approach to problem solving and income creation that gives you the freedom to get paid to do things in a way that suits the person you are, and create an amazing lifestyle in the process.

This is what makes free ranging different to a regular old 'business' (and very different to a job!): while most traditional businesses (and careers) require you to fit yourself into them in order to make things work, the free range approach is all about crafting something to fit *your* personality and priorities... so you don't have to leave a piece of yourself at the door in order to get paid anymore.

Sounds completely crazy? I agree: a few years ago, making a living without a proper job (and especially doing it as you) was a crazy far-off dream that only a 'lucky' few achieved, but now things are different. Many people don't know about this new option but those who do are poking their heads out of the career cage, blinking in the sunlight and flapping their wings to a better, free range life. You can too (and this book shows you how).

Why this is possible now

We are living at a remarkable point in history. Right now, you can make a living from pretty much anything you can imagine. In the last decade alone, technology has zoomed forward beyond anything your college career adviser thought possible *and beyond anything you read in the job ads*:

- Today, you can run a global seminar without even getting out of bed.

- You can pack your entire business in your backpack and take off around the world (while still seeing money drop into your bank account).

- You can reach thousands of people and create a consistent income in ways that were unimaginable 20 years ago.

- You can get going fast without going to a single early morning networking meeting (unless that's your thing!).

- You can have an idea, draw it out, and launch in under two weeks...

Crucially, you can do this right now without even quitting your job. Starting this evening – from the comfort of your kitchen table – you can experiment, run a 'test project', and start with the ideas in this book *before* deciding to say goodbye to the boss. This is how I quit my last-ever job and how hundreds of other free rangers do it too. (Of course, if you have to change things sooner, we have options to help with that too!)

Never before has it been possible to go from idea to income so easily, but most people still don't know how to make this work (I certainly didn't when I was in my career cage). Here's why:

The gap between assumptions and reality

A few years ago, I was on a boat trip to some beautiful islands in southern Thailand. Clear blue waters, cavorting monkeys on islands and endless snorkelling. On the boat I met lovely people, most of whom had jobs back in the 'real world'. They spoke of how they would love to stay here forever instead of going back to the office at the end of their vacation. Over the course of the day one person made three comments that stuck in my mind. These comments contain common assumptions about work – see if you can identify them:

1 *About herself*: 'I guess the good thing about working in the corporate world is that you can afford to visit beautiful places like this.'

2 *About the boat captain*: 'He must be doing well. That's the life. Move to Thailand and get rich off a boat company. Maybe he can hire me!'

3 *About me*: 'Being able to write and travel must be nice. Do you work in pubs or something to keep going?'

Did you identify the assumptions?

Assumption 1. You have to work in a job to get to visit beautiful places and have a great lifestyle. I hadn't yet told them that I had been hanging out there for four months and hadn't set foot in an office for years.

Assumption 2. Big shiny infrastructure – especially expensive stuff like boats – automatically means a great income. Truth? I spoke to the captain and he confided that even though his tours sell out almost every day, he barely breaks even. The costs simply don't work – the boat makes him look 'rich' but the fuel and the staff don't come for free (so no, he isn't going to hire her).

Assumption 3.   If you don't have a job and don't have a business that revolves around something you can touch (such as boats) then you're little better than unemployed. You must be broke. That's the killer assumption, and part of what we are going to challenge in this book.

What I'm going to show you is how to figure out what you want, create a life that suits you down to the ground, and build a great income doing it. The strategies you'll learn don't depend on you owning boats, but they do give you the freedom to hang about diving off them as much as you like.

Welcome to the Third Way

Free ranging is the Third Way between jobs and high-risk entrepreneurship. This is a new game, with new rules. No funding, no big risky investment, no premises or staff, but bags of personality, play and freedom: that's a free range business. I'm going to show you simple ways to start with what you have, and create a free range income that *more than replicates your monthly pay cheque* (but gives you way more freedom and fulfilment).

This book shows that you have options other than staying with the way things are for the rest of your days. Which rather begs the question:

What do you really want to do with your life?

I'm betting that at least once in the last year you've tried to figure out your 'dream job'. I'm also betting you haven't *quite* settled on one answer yet.

Here's how it usually works: you struggle for years to identify one perfect job. After much searching, maybe you find it, fantastic!

You've discovered your dream career! Now, you'd better hope you're qualified for it, hope it pays enough, and hope the employer agrees to take you on. If you get past those hurdles (which most don't), the next step is to squeeze the entirety of your rich, complex personality and dreams into that one tiny job description and give up on the bits that don't fit. Then, you'd better hope you'll still love it five years down the line – because you don't want to go through all *that* again.

Tra la. Your dream job. Congratulations.

Doesn't that sound less than ideal to you?

The truth is that you are way more interesting and complex than a single job description. As a Free Range Human, you get to *create* your own dream career when no one job ticks the boxes. You decide where you spend your days, what you do, and how you do it. You can combine several interests tailored to suit your unique personality. No more packing yourself into a box.

What's more, free range career change is easier than changing fields in the job world. You don't have to convince an employer to take you on and you don't need a perfectly matching résumé/CV. A Free Range Human can build status in a new field quickly, make the move to pretty much anything that takes their fancy, and constantly evolve that as they grow and change.

In this book you're not going to search aimlessly for your dream solution; you're going to learn how to grab the reins and *create* it. The payoff? Your life, lived in full colour every day.

You can join us

The free range tribe is growing and we'd love you to join us. This isn't a pipe dream reserved for the 'lucky ones'. More and more people are discovering that life no longer has to be a choice between trapped and well-off versus free and broke. I'm going to lift the lid and show you how real career-cage escapes happen and how you can do it too.

What you will discover

In this book you will learn:

- How to figure out what you really want to do with your life (and create your own bespoke 'dream career').

- How to tweak any idea to suit your personality so you don't have to squeeze yourself into another box.

- How to get paid *more* by being more you.

- How to make this happen *without* an idea for a world-changing widget.

- How to test an idea and get going without even quitting your job.

- How to go from zero to 'go-to' person in your industry in months.

- How to start for the price of a new pair of shoes, with no funding (ie no debt), and get your first project out there in two weeks.

- How to stand out from the crowd (and get paid what you deserve).

- How to find ways to make things work in line with *your* personality and strengths.

- How to fast-track your journey to get better results in six months than many old-style businesses achieve in six years.

- More to the point, you'll learn how to create a lifestyle you truly love... while earning an income that more than pays the bills.

In the first half of this book (Parts 1 and 2), you'll figure out what you want. Then, in Parts 3 and 4, you'll start to hatch your escape plan.

What this book is not

Before you think that I'm going to paint some crazy vision of quitting your job, finding some dodgy 'money-making scheme' and

Think like a Free Range Human

Don't look for the perfect example of someone exactly in your situation who made the exact move you're thinking of making. You simply won't find them: look hard enough and there will *always* be a reason why someone's situation was different, and always a reason why it might not be possible. The question is, are you going to choose to let that stop you?

Remember, no one who made their escape is any better than you. Free rangers are not smarter, richer, younger, older or more attractive; they don't have a certain career history, and their situation is not down to fate. Fate is what happens when you get up and do things other people thought they could only achieve when 'luck' came knocking.

My journey from stressed career-cage worker to Free Range Human was not about luck or connections, it was down to thinking like a free ranger and learning about this new world's possibilities. Possibilities that, back then, I didn't even know were out there. In this book, you're going to discover them too. We're going to explore, have fun and bust you out of there.

Part One
Get ready for the ride

01
What your school career adviser never told you

The 'safe job' myth

I need to pay the bills therefore I need to keep my job. It's fine to dream but you have to get back to reality.

As one stuck career cager said: 'When I start thinking about making the change, what goes through my head is a whole heap of reasons not to jump. We need a steady income; what happens if it goes wrong and I can't pay the bills?'

If you want to provide for your family (or your cat), and not end up homeless in a cardboard box, then reality says to stay put.

Myth buster

Up until recently, most people made a deal: 'I'll work (in a job I don't necessarily love) in return for a salary I can rely on.' The aim was a job for life: work all day and then play on weekends and in retirement.

But then, work hours started getting longer and jobs stopped being safe. Look at your employment contract right now: what's your notice period? One month? Three months? That's exactly how much security you have. Don't kid yourself that you have permanence.

Of course, the job-for-life generation also told us that if we worked hard we'd end up with a great retirement. If we stuck at that soul-sapping job, when we were 60 we could live fabulously, travel and have a whale of a time (assuming we made it that far).

But wait a minute… didn't those same retirement plans go down the tube in the last big financial crash? Where thousands upon thousands of people who had worked their whole life for the dream at the end were left stranded?

More to the point, analysts are now predicting that a large percentage of the population won't be able to retire until their seventies or eighties.[1] A long time to wait. *That career-cage deal isn't looking so hot now.* This is the new reality of the workplace. The question is: are you still playing by the old rules?

The old rules

Jobs have not always been the default way to make a living. Prior to the Industrial Revolution in the late 1800s, working for yourself was seen as a normal and laudable pursuit. However, when factories emerged, priorities changed. Factories needed compliant workers to follow the rules. Soon, innovation, individuality and creative thinking were no longer seen as valuable skills for the majority of the population.

That's how we created our career-cage workers all those years ago: cogs in a factory, and then the factory became an office. *Do your job, don't ask questions. Work isn't something you're meant to enjoy.* We were taught to be competent, comply and you'll have a good career.

Then, all of a sudden, the old rules stopped working.

Jobs started to become automated. Today, a computer can do the work of a dozen people in roles as varied as data entry, engineering and even law. As that change shook the world, the internet came along and globalization took off. Jobs across previously untouchable industries were being farmed out to India, China and whoever would do it the cheapest. Then, as uncertainty around the world grew, many of the jobs left were consolidated. I bet you know at least one person who is now covering the workload previously shouldered by two people.

(And that's even *before* we talk about what's ahead with AI (artificial intelligence)).[2] Suddenly, the game changed. And the myth of the safe job changed with it.

Jobs are a not always the smartest idea in this economy

Here's why:

1 **Jobs are risky**. With job security out the window for most people, employment is the equivalent to being self-employed with *only one client* (your employer). And as any business expert will tell you, being 100 per cent dependent on one client, in a turbulent market, is a very risky business. If they get into trouble, there goes your income.

2 **Someone else is in control of your life**. As an employee, the reality is that you have little control over the source of your income. Call me crazy, but I don't want someone else to determine whether I get my next pay cheque or end up on the streets.

   I notice that many of my friends in jobs are afraid of the economy and nervous about what 'the board' is going to decide next. In contrast, my free range friends see any change as an opportunity (indeed many of the greatest companies in the world were created by entrepreneurs who seized the moment in downturns).[3]

   You see, this is not about escaping a job once. It's about the freedom that comes when you know how to make money on your own terms. *True freedom is being able to dance with the changes rather than being a victim to your circumstances.*

3 Jobs can suck. When you work a job, odds are someone else has control of what you do, when you work, what you earn, what you work on, and when you are allowed to take a day off. You abdicate choice over what you do every day for most of your life in exchange for a pay cheque. This is the 'employment compromise'.

With jobs less secure than ever and free range incomes easier to create than at any other time in history, does this compromise really make sense?

While everyone around you simultaneously complains about their job and is terrified of losing it, here's how to get free and get happy.

What a free range business looks like:

- no funding or debt needed;
- you can start now for the price of a few dinners out;
- based on your personality, what you love and the life you want;
- playful, flexible and able to change as you do.

Perfect for right now: affordable to start, super profitable and you can mould it around you. The truth is that there's no reason why you have to work for someone else if you don't want to. Fabulous adventures and a lifetime of discovery await outside that door.

Wait, don't the majority of small businesses fail?

This is the showstopper. You get all excited about the possibilities... and then you hear this. *Splat.* With that one line, any dreams of breaking free are dashed. Problem is, that 'fact' simply is not true. Duncan Bannatyne, serial entrepreneur and star of the UK's *Dragons' Den*, points out:

> *A lot of people don't want to have to face family and friends who were always sceptical of their chances of success. They've probably*

heard the statistic that 50 per cent of businesses fail in their first two years, but this statistic is usually based on the closure of business bank accounts, NOT the close of businesses.

If you remove the number of businesses that change bank accounts when introductory deals run out, or the number of businesses that are wound up because the founder took up a lucrative job offer, or started another business, the so-called failure rate drops dramatically.

Barclays' New Business Division estimates that the number of businesses that close because of 'external financial stress', ie owing money, is just 12 per cent in the first year.[4]

Saying that a business failed because someone moved on is like saying anyone who quit their job and moved on to another one 'failed' at that job (even if they left to take a promotion). Ridiculous right?

Yes, of course some businesses do 'fail' in the conventional sense – but between you and me, one look at their website and approaches usually makes it pretty clear why. This is not about random luck. There are specific things to do to ensure this works. We are going to explore those in the second half of the book; and remember, with a free range business you're not sinking in loads of money and putting your house on the line! You're starting small – you can even get going while still in your job (or existing business) – and playing it out to create a tailor-made career that you love, that *more* than pays the bills. For now, consider this:

Free range third way

The question is, do you want to *feel* secure, or *be* secure?

The reality is that neither option, job or free range, is ever going to be 100 per cent secure. No option ever is. What matters is that when change happens (and it will) are you positioned as a potential victim or a potential winner?

There is an irony here. A job feels secure while a business does not. It feels secure to get a pay cheque – and those big glass buildings look to be so real and solid. But the reality is that going free range gives you that sort of lifetime security that an employee imagines they have – *until the moment they realize they really, really don't.*

Put that way, ask yourself again: 'Can I afford to escape the 9–5?' This time also ask yourself: 'Can I afford not to?'

02
Why this matters now

Three weeks after I left my teens, my mum died from cancer.
Yes, I still miss her, and no it doesn't get any easier.

Her passing left me with a strong awareness of the shortness of life. Across the top of my laptop are words, *One life, baby. One life.* Every morning I look at those words and remember the real stakes here.

What would you do if you had only one life?

(You do, you know.)

If you get one thing from this book, get this: stop kidding yourself that you have 300 years to live. 'Someday' is code for never; 'one day' is the path for taking your dreams to the grave with you.

There will never be a 'right time' to make the change. Everyone thinks they are too old or too young, too poor or too well paid, too attached or too single – and certainly too busy. The truth is that there never will be a perfect time, age or situation.

There are also no second chances.

Except the one you give yourself, starting today.

Part One reflections – where I am now

I picked up this book because: _____

_____

_____

_____

Of what I have read so far, what resonated with me is: _____

_____

_____

_____

The things I don't enjoy about my current work life are: _____

_____

_____

_____

I have been dreaming of making a change for _____

_____ months/years

It is important for me to make a change because: _____

_____

_____

_____

The biggest question I have right now is: _____

_____

_____

_____

Notes

1 Canada Life Group (UK) (2017) Record number of employees to work beyond 65, 10 May, https://www.canadalife.co.uk/news/employees-to-work-beyond-65-press-release;

Shaw, V (2016) Workers may need to retire as late as 81 to get a pension like their parents, report warns, *Independent, 2 March*, https://www.independent.co.uk/news/business/news/pension-age-retire-royal-london-westminster-81-a6906676.html;

Career Builder (2017) Half of mature US Workers will wait until at least age 70 to retire or won't retire at all, 31 March, http://press.careerbuilder.com/2017-03-31-Half-of-Mature-U-S-Workers-Will-Wait-Until-At-Least-Age-70-to-Retire-or-Wont-Retire-at-All

2 Harari, Y N (2018) In the long run no job will remain absolutely safe from automation, in *21 Lessons for the 21st Century*, Spiegel & Grau, New York

3 Burn-Callander, R (2014) Recession start-ups are more profitable, *Telegraph*, 2 September, https://www.telegraph.co.uk/finance/businessclub/sales/11068457/Recession-start-ups-are-more-profitable.html

4 Bannatyne, D (2008) *Wake Up And Change Your Life*, Orion, London

Part Two
Creating your free range life

How to decide what you really want

suggests that the point isn't loving the work you do, it is to find a 'muse' (low-time-commitment business) that lets you work as few hours as possible for maximum return on your time. I'm totally behind that last part! But the assumption that you don't need to love what you do to get there is questionable.

Ferris's own 'muse' was a sports supplements venture, and as he explains in his second book, improving how the body works is his biggest interest. He first became known for his approach to finding the most efficient way to get results: something he is passionate about doing every day in his own life. His and other people's successes were not ideas plucked from the air with no relation to their personality or interests.

Doing what you love is not only, you know, *kind of the point of doing this*, but it is your route to making it a success. If you don't love doing something, then unless you have superhuman willpower, I guarantee you will end up dropping it no matter how smart a concept it is. I've seen hundreds of perfectly good ideas dropped when someone chose them because they were 'clever', not because they were really, genuinely into them.

Save yourself time and get honest about what you want upfront. The next exercise gets you thinking along these lines. Take time now to scribble your answers to the nine questions.

Exercise: The nine questions

Brain dump your answers to these questions. No second guessing or self-editing, just get a pen and write:

1   When you were about eight years old, the three things you could generally be found doing for play were:

   _____

   _____

2 The last time you felt alive and completely engaged in the moment was when? Where?

_____

_____

3 Imagine a genie appeared and offered you 12 months off – with full pay and the security of knowing your job would be waiting for you when you get back. You have a whole year just to do stuff that excites you. What would you do?

Write your answer from the first month to the last (use another notebook if you run out of space here):

_____

_____

4 Make a note: what is it about each part of your 12 months off that's really exciting to you? For example, if you wrote that you would create art, are you excited about actually making art, or about the place you imagined doing it, or about the people you imagined doing it with?

_____

_____

Don't worry if you're unsure of your answers. These questions are intended to just get your brain into gear for free ranging. In a few chapters' time you can come back to this with a lot more clarity.

The next five questions are a safe place to capture those 'one day' thoughts that might be going through your head. Consider what you think would be awesome to do if only you had all the permission/experience you needed and knew it would not fail.

5 Three things I would love to do as a free range career are:

_____

_____

6 What excites me about each idea is:

_____

_____

7 What holds me back from each idea is:

_____

_____

8 When I try to make a change I generally:

_____

_____

9 If I had the guts I would (Really. What would you do?):

_____

_____

Remember: you're not bound to anything you write, so don't hold back.

Now, take a look at what usually goes on when you try to make a change (question 8). Are your usual responses to changing your work throwing up more barriers than solutions? To help you do things differently, here's how to get around a common barrier on the road to discovering what to do with your life: the Idea–Death Cycle.

My client Sam spent months in this cycle: she would come up with an idea and then, within seconds, the voice of that inner critic would wipe it out with a cry of 'unfeasible'! Then she would start again: find an idea she liked, think of a reason why not to do it, and go round and round in circles.

That's the way to end up stuck in that office forever. As you'll learn in this book, most ideas don't start out great, they grow that way when given room to breathe. _No one goes from 'I don't know what I want to do' to 'Here is the answer together with a bullet-proof business plan' in one fell swoop!_

To give yourself the best chance of coming up with a great idea that a) you'll love and b) will work, use this simple technique:

The two-step strategy

The mistake Sam was making was trying to land on an idea that was both *attractive and feasible* all in one go. If it wasn't both, she would give up. However, trying to nail down the practical details the very moment you come up with creative ideas is the fastest way to kill off your very best ideas.

As Professor Richard Wiseman explains in summing up leading research into creativity, your methodical and critical mind (the conscious brain) is like the loud man in the room. The creative (unconscious) part of your brain is the quiet man – the one that is super-smart and comes up with the stickiest ideas. Problem is, the quiet man backs down the second the loud man starts shouting out reasons why not.[3]

If you want to discover what you really want, you have to give the quiet, innovative mind some space. Here's how to do it.

Use the two-step strategy to separate your dreams from what, at this stage, you think is possible. Step 1: nail down what you want. Step 2: figure out what works, and make it possible.

To help you do this I've separated this book into several sections. This part is exclusively Step 1 thinking. *This is your safe place to dream, and dream big. No idea is too wild in this space.* Don't worry, we'll get to the practicalities and checks later (I'm not here to let you go off with a bad idea!) but right now you have full permission to let down the guard and get dreaming.

By starting with the focus on *you* – bringing you alive, getting your brain buzzing with free range potential and filling you with possibilities – we're opening up avenues that linear thinking would never even reach.

Get ready for the ride

The following pages are packed with concepts and techniques that have had the most success in the real world. While some pages might feel a bit 'touchy feely', believe me, I have no patience with pointless fluff. If something is included in this book it is here for a simple reason: it works. *But only if you let it.*

So here's the deal: for the next few chapters, trust in the process, OK? At the end, any objections you have will be waiting and you are free to reclaim them, but for now, all I ask is that you dive in and give it your all. In return, I'll show you a whole new way of seeing your options. Deal?

Brilliant. Let's get started.

04
Dream big – then get off your butt and do it

'You can't wait for inspiration. You have to go after it with a club.'

JACK LONDON

Dan was an intelligent man who showed up to one of my courses. I asked him, 'What would you do if you could do anything, anything at all?' He replied, 'Well, I guess I'd work a little bit less, have a bit more time, and not have to do as many spreadsheets.'

A *little* less? A *little* more time? Not do *as much* of something that makes your heart sink? When this is the best dream someone can come up with... you know something has gone seriously wrong. You know that saying, 'Aim for the sky and you'll reach the ceiling; aim for the ceiling and you'll stay on the floor'?[4] That's exactly what's happening here.

Want a dream life? It's time to remember how to dream BIG, which is the exact opposite of how the world of work has taught you to behave. So I'd like to show you an example of what can happen when you dare to dream, free range style.

05
Defrosting – your secret weapon in figuring out what you want

'The intuitive mind is a sacred gift and the rational mind is a faithful servant. We have created a society that honours the servant and has forgotten the gift.'

ALBERT EINSTEIN

Clara came up to me after a workshop. The moment I saw her I felt the stress. She was rigid and tense, and throughout the workshop she had been feverishly taking notes. She pushed her glasses back up her nose, and said, 'I liked everything you said but I didn't get an answer from the exercises. Is there some sort of test I can do that will tell me what I should do with my life?'

I asked Clara how she had got on with the 'Head in the Clouds' exercise. She opened her notebook (with the name of a major law firm emblazoned on the front), flicked through her notes before looking up, tears welling: 'I couldn't think of anything I wanted to do except sit on the beach and do nothing!'

'That's OK,' I said. 'How about the question on the last time you felt really alive?'

Clara shook her head sadly and said, 'I don't remember. Isn't that stupid? I remember everything else in my life: dates of meetings, names of clients, but I can't remember the last time I felt alive. Is there something wrong with me?'

There was nothing wrong with Clara. Only, it wasn't Clara completing those exercises. The real Clara was frozen, deep down inside the efficient lawyer-Clara. She bubbled up in the moments where Clara would unexpectedly burst into tears but disappeared again when lawyer-Clara berated her for being so silly. *Lawyer-Clara could be a bit of a bitch.*

Lawyer-Clara was great at her work; she knew how to get a promotion and handle a complex case. But she was absolutely terrible at figuring out what would make real Clara happy. She toned it down, reminded herself to 'be careful not to mess up her résumé', tried to 'logic' her way to every decision and, in the process, kept Clara away from the single most useful tool for figuring out what she really wanted: her internal GPS.

Your internal GPS is a term used by author and coach Martha Beck to describe that feeling you get when, say, you're about to go into a relationship with someone who turns out to be Really Very Wrong for you, or that 'no!' feeling you get on the first day at that job that turns out to be a bad environment.[6] You *knew* they were wrong, but you couldn't explain why. They looked good on paper. If you're like me (or Clara) you probably said, 'Don't be so silly, it's just a feeling, I can't turn down the job/leave them'. So you went ahead with the 'yes' when your body was screaming 'no'. *And we both know how that worked out.*

Is your GPS out of whack?

I was speaking with my friend, the fabulous life design coach Selina Barker, about this topic, and she pointed out that:

At a very early age young kids are vocal about what they want – very firm in their yeses and nos and I wants. Then as they grow up, they're told 'you can't have that'. So we learn to say no where we wanted to say yes.

Now, as you go through this book and come across ideas, tap back into that internal GPS. How are you responding? What signals are you getting? Remember there is no point wasting time on an option if you get a big screaming 'no!' inside. That one never works out. By learning to listen to how you're feeling you can shortcut the process of figuring out what you really want, and tap into that really-right path much faster.

06

How to create your perfect 'career' when you want to do everything

'Ideas are like rabbits. You get a couple and learn to handle them, and pretty soon you have a dozen.'

JOHN STEINBECK

In the previous chapter we explored some ways of tapping into your dreams. But what do you do when you have lots of little dreams yet no *single* thing that grabs you enough to choose it above the others?

When I was starting out, I had trouble deciding what I wanted. There were so many ideas for things I'd love to do, lives I'd want to live, but I couldn't choose. No one idea was perfect and I didn't want to make the wrong decision (again) or close the door on another option.

Since then I've heard the same problem from many clients:

If I launch this consulting business in my home town then I'll miss out on my dream of living in Bali teaching meditation. Also I've always wanted to make documentaries. And breed cats. Maybe. I have no idea how to choose!

Every time you come close to choosing, you worry that you'll get bored after a month. So you give up... until the next time that your work becomes unbearable. Then the cycle starts again: you fantasize about another life, read a book for inspiration, dare to dream for just a minute... then get stuck. You can't see how to answer the question: 'How can I get someone to pay me to do everything I love?'

Familiar?

Welcome to the 'one thing' myth.

The 'one thing' myth

'I need to choose one thing to do for the rest of my life and I can't start until I find that one perfect job title.'

Myth buster

I just want to get one thing clear here: I think the whole concept of choosing 'one path' off the shelf, and sticking to it for the rest of your life, is just nuts. *Totally bonkers.*

You wouldn't assume that you could choose one outfit to wear every day, for every occasion, for the rest of your life and be happy with it. So why assume you can do the same with a career? This is why a lot of people get stuck at the 'deciding' stage. You're looking at all these 'options' out there and putting a lot of pressure on *one* of them being perfect.

Free Range Humans do things differently. They don't expect to find that perfect 'forever outfit'. Instead, they create their own bespoke career, from scratch, by thinking outside the job box. You see:

You *don't* have to get paid directly for something to make it a core part of your business.

If you're a consultant, you won't spend each hour of every day consulting. If you teach people organic gardening, you're not going to run organic gardening classes all day.

For example:

- *I don't make my living by being paid to hang out in cafés.* Sitting in cake dens with my laptop, watching the comings and goings, breathing in the aroma, and chatting to lovely people is one of my favourite things, and a core part of my working day. Yet I'm *not* running a café.

- *I don't make my living by getting paid to teach psychology, social anthropology and linguistics.* Almost everything I do is focused on these very elements: they form a big part of the Free Range Humans approach. Yet no one has *paid* me to be a linguist or a social anthropologist.

- *I don't make my living by being paid to write.* Yes I'm writing a book but that isn't a full-time income (and it was also the first time I agreed to get paid directly to write!). However, I've been writing, every week, as part of my business for years. At the start, it was guest articles and posts (which brought in traffic), as well as courses, and stories that illustrate my Free Range e-mails – time and time again I manage to write and tell stories in a way I love and this fun project has grown my business massively.

- *I don't get paid to travel the world.* Over the last few years I've travelled to places like Bali, Costa Rica, France, Italy, Mauritius, the Philippines and Australia and run my business from there. This book was written in five different countries (and most of the updates to this new edition were made in sunny California – my new home base!). Yet no one is paying me to travel.

- *I don't get paid to meet incredible people, be enthusiastic or do creative photo and video projects.* But I integrate these into my day and they enhance what I do get paid for (a portfolio career that includes freeing career-cage-trapped humans!).

There's a myth out there that the only way to do what you love as a career is to get paid directly for that activity. Kind of like in a job (which is most people's only model of making an income). So, if you like travel and writing, the career-cage answer is to be a travel writer (like thousands of others out there). If you can't get that, then you have to give up.

But working for yourself is not like having a job – when you're free range, the thing you get paid for directly is often not what takes up the bulk of your time. Ask anyone who does well as a solopreneur, and they will say that *growing their business* is a core part of how they spend their days. Some people (conventional business types) find this part boring. Free Range Humans see it as an excuse for getting playful.

To grow your business, you might end up writing, filming, giving talks, baking cakes (I know someone who did this as a promotional idea!), meeting lots of fascinating people (the ones currently on your 'dream dinner' list), or an endless range of other options. With no boss to set the agenda, you get to choose what you do.

Knowing this, here are three out-of-the-box approaches you can use to create your perfect free range solution:

1 Create a bespoke career.

2 Create a portfolio career.

3 Create an evolving career.

1. Create a bespoke career

Have you ever walked into a clothes shop, seen a mannequin with an outfit that looks amazing, and tried on the whole thing from top to toe? I have. It didn't look right at all. It's one thing to get inspiration from the shop floor, but then you need to add that scarf, remove those boots, find a different top... and then it looks just perfect.

The truth is that you are unique. Perfect-fit careers are not 'found'; they are created from scratch, tweaked and tailor-made to suit you in all your uniqueness.

When I became a coach, I realized I didn't exactly love everything about coaching. For example, I'm not one to sit back, listen and nod while someone car-crashes their life, or restrain enthusiasm when it's clear you've hit on something fabulous. For months I was so stressed about this: every session I felt like I had to pretend to be someone else (someone more passive) in order to fit the box of the conventional coaching world. I felt as if I wasn't good enough because I was different.

So, after spending too long packing my personality into a box, I decided to turn my natural style into an advantage – not hide it, out of fear it might be a liability.

I came out as myself, as your feisty Free Range Humans guide. Now, it's less 'and what do *you* think?' and more strategies, ideas, brainstorming inspiration and a dose of straight talking (with love). I joke, I laugh, I ask the big questions, I say it like it is. Occasionally I swear. *Try finding that in a job description.*

Result? *Way* happier. To my surprise, this honesty and new way of connecting with people landed me with a bunch more clients too. This is a common occurrence when free rangers break the rules and come out as themselves rather than following the beige crowd.

Other changes I made (which others said were impossible) include location-freeing a conventionally one-location business, and integrating creativity to promote my business, such as drawing the little chicken logo that still hangs out on the Free Range Humans website. That increases my business and, at the same time, is so much fun I'd do it for free.

Getting the picture? What other people do is not your job description. You can and should tailor ideas to suit you.

Exercise: Tailoring to fit

Steps to tailor free range careers to fit:

1   List your favourite ideas for a free range career.
    These ideas don't need to be perfect, just list the ones you found in some way attractive:

    _____

    _____

2 Identify the elements of each idea that have held you back from choosing that one for sure (ie what about it do you think will not be so fun? What parts of it are you concerned might not suit your personality?).

_____

_____

3 Taking inspiration from my example above, how could you change each idea so that your personality and preferences are a benefit rather than a liability?

_____

_____

4 Look at your ideas list now. Is there any way you can integrate several of your ideas into one solution?
For example, if you are attracted to both X and Y you could potentially combine those to create Z. Brainstorm possible combinations below.

_____

_____

5 Looking back over what you have come up with in steps 3 and 4, is there any option that now seems particularly attractive? Circle the ones you could potentially see yourself moving forward with and getting excited about!

_____

_____

If nothing fits perfectly now, don't worry. Come back to this exercise as you progress throughout this book and get more inspiration. Continue to add to your list and 'tailor' using these techniques until you create a solution that truly ticks your boxes.

Mini case study

I had been a dreamer all my life, but never found a job to match my dreams. For example, I wanted to write about sex but had never found a job that asked for this – especially in the academic circles I had been working in for the previous 10 years. I finally realized that I didn't have to wait for a job to show up – I could create my own role as a sex writer. I set up a business supporting women to enjoy their sexuality – and that led to workshops in beautiful locations, a regular writing slot with the leading magazine in my space, and even my first novel being published. My advice: start small but dream big!

Anna Sansom
www.annasansom.com

2. Create a portfolio career

Can't fit all of your ideas into one solution? You'll love this.

There's a growing tribe of humans out there who get paid to do more than one thing. There's even a name for this: portfolio careers. A portfolio career is where you do more than one type of thing, and get paid for it. You might be a writer, an image consultant and teach yoga. As Barrie Hopson and Katie Ledger point out in their book *And What Do You Do? 10 Steps to Creating a Portfolio Career*, a portfolio career is not the same thing as having a few ideas and not being able to make a success of any one of them – it's a conscious choice that lets you achieve a work blend that fits.

A great example of this is Carla Watkins:

I'd worked for a big finance company for years. I knew deep down that life wasn't for me but while I'd tried a few things in my spare time I didn't see a way out. There was this quiet, heavy feeling of, 'Well this is what adult life is like, you just have to accept it and get on with it'. I couldn't fathom spending my whole life that way, but every time I mentioned these feelings to someone else, they looked at me as though I was speaking gibberish.

So when I came across Free Range Humans online (and this book) I was floored – I wasn't the only one who felt this way. I wasn't broken, I was just in the wrong place.

The concept of a portfolio career stood out to me right away. I've always sought out variety in my life, so work that has a variety of topics made so much sense. How had I not considered this seriously before?

My new portfolio career has included a web design business, a stationery subscription box for people as obsessed with stationery as I am, teaching burlesque classes, be-a-real-mermaid experiences for events and parties (yes that's a real niche!) as well as photography for entrepreneurs. At first, I chose to keep a new (happier!) job I'd moved to as part of my 'portfolio', and evolve the other parts on the side, but today I am full-time as my own boss, with my own unique mix.

As Carla says, had she tried to find the *one* perfect thing to do, she never would have started:

especially with something like my stationery box business, as I wasn't sure it would be 'enough' alone. But by including it as part of my portfolio career this side project had room to grow and I'm still doing it today.[8]

The wonderful thing about a portfolio career is that, just like Carla, you get to edit your career when you get bored – you can add in one strand today that you decide to wind down a year later, and you can replace that with something else, without going through a huge career change.

Mini case study

I used to define myself by my job title and the company I worked for – but now if someone asks me 'What do you do?', I *love* the fact that I can say 'I do a few things actually... I'm an HR consultant, photographer, executive coach and also a school governor'. It's nice to be openly multi-dimensional. I feel much 'freer', and since making the move from career cage to free range I'm earning as much if not more than I was before but only working for half the time, meaning I can spend more precious time with my family.

Frank Mason

3. Create an evolving career

Becoming a Free Range Human isn't like a career change into another 'job sector'. You don't have to choose one business and stick to that, and *only* that, for 10 years.

The truth is that if you're someone who loves variety and change, odds are you would never be happy doing one thing, and only one thing, forever. So quit pretending that's even an option for you. I was chatting about this with the wonderful Barbara Winter, author of *Making A Living Without A Job.*[9] Barbara has been self-employed for over 40 years and has had more strands to her career than most people have ideas.

'Who said you had to do one thing for the rest of your life?' she asked. 'You're choosing for this year's version of you, not the 10 years in the future version of you. Who *knows* what that person will want?'

When you learn how to be a Free Range Human, you're learning the tools to launch whatever you like, and edit your business so it continues to grow with you. You're building a flexible vessel for your life, so choosing the right general direction of the vessel is all that matters: you can correct the details along the way.

A single job in which you do just one thing? Squeezing yourself into someone else's job description? Outdated. Now *you* have control. When no one job fits, it's time to create your own bespoke free range career.

Exercise: Reflection

What have you realized from this chapter? Capture your thoughts about each option in the table below:

Table 6.1   Reflection

	Why I find this attractive	How I could use this
1 Bespoke career		
2 Portfolio career	eg because I have two ideas I am keen to do and couldn't decide between them!	eg start out with consulting in my current field while building up my idea for public-speaking workshops
3 Evolving career		

Resources

For more on choosing what you want and creating a bespoke career, get my free audio on 'How to Create Your Own Career When No One Job Fits' at https://frh.me/doeverything

Free range action

Get a taste of free range life

Connie Solera, a Free Range Human you'll meet later in this book, says:

> When I decided I was going to go free range, the most powerful thing I did was creating a mini-version of the life I wanted while still in my job. I wasn't ready to quit there and then, but while I was getting ready, I could change who I spent time with. So I made a point of avoiding the negative people in the office. When I had to see them, I would politely refuse to get drawn in to their negative conversations.
>
> I did other things, like taking a day off and going to a café with my laptop, and doing exactly what I imagined I would do on a free range day. In the evenings I made time to create art: that was all part of my dream picture.
>
> These actions got me into the mindset of making up my own rules. You can't come up with ideas and just dream about them, you have to live them.

Many other free rangers have similar stories. For example, in the months before leaving my last job I got permission to get out and work on a project by myself in the downstairs Starbucks. Sure it was a chain in an underground shopping mall but this taste of free range life made a big difference. I asked for permission 'just this once', and then it turned into a regular assumption that I would pop down there once every few days.

These actions help you become aware of what does and does not work for you, and many people find that shaking up their routine allows for unexpected ideas to show up. It also gives you a taste of creating the life you want, like a real Free Range Human.

Now it's your turn. Change something in your life this week to bring it in line with your dream. For example, if 'variety' is one of your themes, do something as small as taking a new route to work. If spending time with certain types of people came up as important, find them (be it through friends or discovering an event where they gather), and get out of your usual circles for an hour this week.

What are three free range actions you could take over the next three weeks?

_____

_____

Which one do you want to make happen this week?

_____

_____

Hint: If you think an action is too inaccessible, simply ask, 'How would a Free Range Human make this happen?' and go and do that.

Mini case study

When I first picked up this book I had the sort of job you 'just don't quit'. But secretly that's all I wanted to do. Problem was, at first I didn't know what else to do or how to get there. I am a responsible person, a real planner and I wasn't going to leave right away (even though I wanted to), but one thing I *could* control was my lunch breaks.

So that's what I did. Every day I'd leave the office, even if I was just walking around the block listening to TED talks or exploring potential ideas – for *that* hour every day, I was free range.

It was such a small step. I didn't imagine it would be the snowball that led to an avalanche of changes that ended with me today living and working on my laptop from surf destinations around the world, getting paid to help other people in ways I never saw possible then.

It sounds funny to say 'it started with a lunch break', but it did. Had I just thought about it and not taken the actions I don't think I'd be here today.

Nicole Est

07
Spot your superpowers

'Freedom means finding a home for all your talents.'

SCOTT GINSBERG

There's one more piece of the puzzle to creating your perfect free range solution: *you*. How can you have an above-average – scrap that, a *fabulous* – life if you believe you are nothing but average? Answer: you can't. To create an inspiring free range career, you need to become comfortable with your secret superpowers. Consider this:

1 You are not the sum of your 'learned skills'.

2 You do have something special to offer the world.

3 And you don't have to be the next Mozart for that to be true.

All of this might be a bit different from the way you've been taught to think about yourself so far.

You see, from a young age you've been sold a lie. That lie is that you have to be good at *everything* in order to be 'good enough'. When you were at school and getting that report card, where was the focus: on the subjects you were great at or the ones that 'need work'? If you got private tuition was it for subjects at which you were amazing or the ones that you were not so great at? In the workplace and your annual appraisal, where is the focus?

You know the answer. The focus is always on the weaknesses, about getting you up to average. The bits where you shine, the parts you find natural, those are put to one side. You are 'good enough' at that already, the logic goes. I call this the 'all-rounder' myth.

As a Free Range Human you're going to have to flip that right around. By focusing on your strengths, you tap into your shortcut to loving what you do and standing out in the process.

Average is no longer an option

Mediocrity is what happens when you squash down your greatest strengths in the name of trying to be someone you're not. Ditto with unhappiness, dissatisfaction and the absence of joy. Those feelings all come from disregarding your strengths (because they feel too easy).

Easy does not mean lazy. It simply means you're doing something completely in flow with who you are. The moment you think that something feels too easy and too fun to be of value to others, take note. That's often the moment when people hit upon their greatest thing.

Imagine, just for a moment, if you took all the time you spent struggling against the things you find difficult, tedious and soul-sapping and put *that same time and energy* into doing something that comes naturally to you, something that you do as second nature and that makes you feel wide-awake alive. Imagine how much of an advantage you'd have then. That's why strengths are so important in making a change: tap into your strengths and you can get up to speed in months, rather than battling for years.

'But I already know my strengths and I don't want to use them anymore.'

If you don't like using them, they're not strengths. When we talk about strengths, we're not talking about them in the sense of the way the word is used in the workplace, where strengths are often used to mean 'something you are pretty good at'.

There's a difference between strengths and skills. Skills are something you've learned (and got good at). You don't necessarily love them. Strengths are innate: you have always done them in one form or another (these are your natural points of excellence).

For example, Jill and Dave are both good at corporate presentations. They have both learned the skills involved and can do them well. However, do they *both* have a strength of speaking in public?

From a young age, Jill has always grabbed the microphone and loved being in front of an audience. In contrast, Dave doesn't particularly love doing this; however, he has put in a lot of time and effort to the point where he is fine with it and gets nice feedback. Here's the difference: when Jill gets off the stage her energy is sky high, she can't imagine being anywhere else and is buzzing for days! When Dave gets off the stage he feels drained. He's proud that he did a good job... but he's happy it's over. Jill's best results come when people see her on stage. Dave's best results come from his detailed analysis at his desk. Jill and Dave both have the skill of giving corporate presentations, but Jill has the strength of being a natural speaker.

You can tell the difference between your own skills and strengths in this way. If it's just a skill it'll always feel like a bit of a struggle, even when you get good at it. Also, you won't think, 'I can't believe people *pay* me to do something this fun!'

This is what makes your true strengths so hard to spot; it feels too easy so you might well overlook it. For example, my client Alex was a natural people person; it was blindingly obvious to me that his 'best thing' was bringing together a team. He did it without thinking, and both in and out of work he loved nothing more than making sure everyone was getting on. However, Alex worked in a highly technical field, so he put all his energy into getting good at his technical skills; he didn't believe there was any point talking about his people-based strengths. One day I asked him, 'How do you feel about the people who get paid to manage groups?' He replied, 'I look down on those sorts of roles, to be honest. What they do is fun, it's not real work.' I then put him in touch with another client who had opposite strengths and who, despite years of 'skills training' in people management, still found the people side of the job to be a struggle. That was when Alex realized that what was 'easy and fun' for him was a valuable asset to others.

Alex is not alone. When I work with clients, I can almost guarantee that the very thing they say is 'not that valuable' is the biggest thing they have to offer. This happens because the dominant view of work in our culture is shaped by the Anglo-Saxon Protestant work ethic, which tells us that for something to be worthwhile it has to be hard.[10] This means we habitually disregard our own very best thing for being 'too easy', or we assume that 'everyone can do that'. The truth is that you're not like other people. For each thing you would poke your eye out to avoid, other people are right now reading a copy of this book to try to figure out how to get *paid* to do just that.

The final indicator of a strength is that you're doing it already (even if you don't notice). Although Alex assumed he had risen through the ranks because of his technical skills, he soon realized all his most satisfying successes came back to the way he pulled a team together and made lasting connections. Once you discover your hidden superpowers, a lot of your backstory will make much more sense (and your future path will clear up as well).

So how can you find your strengths? Simple: identify your weaknesses.

Weaknesses are just strengths in the wrong environment

This is such an important point: it's quite possible that the very parts of your personality that you try to hide away at work are the parts that hold the key to your hidden superpowers.

For example, before I changed career back in the job world, I thought I had a huge weakness of constantly wanting to change how things were done. I came up with new ideas all the time for how we could improve the status quo. My boss wasn't interested:

he wanted me to focus on the job at hand, which had nothing to do with creating change. My constant need to make things bigger and better – and never settling for average – was a weakness when I was supposed to just keep things ticking over quietly.

Then, I changed career into consultancy. Suddenly my job was to see how things could be done differently, push the status quo, come up with big ideas. That old weakness, which I had spent years trying to keep down, became a strength that businesses were paying a lot of money for! Plus, I got better results in the first month than I had in years of painstakingly trying to 'get good enough' at something that was against my nature. This was *fun*.

You have several masked strengths in your life, too. Let's say you've been kicking yourself for not being able to focus on just one thing: you bounce between projects too fast, and feel like you can't focus. However, your job tells you to settle down, do one thing at a time, so you're always berating yourself for being like that....

Now imagine an environment where that *exact trait* is a benefit.

I'll tell you a place where this would be an advantage: a brainstorming session. Being able to move between options fast – and not get bogged down in details – is a huge advantage in brainstorming. Turns out that weakness ('being unfocused') was masking the strengths of being able to be a fast-moving, adaptable, big-picture thinker with lots of ideas.

Voila. We have just turned your weakness into a strength.

Exercise: Flip it

To find your hidden strengths, follow these four steps to fill out the table:

1   Write out five things that you currently think of as weaknesses. Include things you can't help doing, tell yourself you should stop doing, or wish you could change and do better.

2 Next, ask yourself: 'What is really behind this weakness?'
*As in the example above, if your weakness is 'I can't focus on
one project at a time', the driver behind that might be 'I love
constant stimulation and my mind moves fast'. Getting to the
personality trait behind the 'weakness' lets you think about it
in a more balanced way.*

3 Now scribble down two situations where each of these traits
would be an advantage.
*In the example above, this was the brainstorming session.
Remember these situations don't have to be 'viable career
options', the point is to know they exist. This step gets your
mind moving to discover possibilities where you can add
value by being you.*

4 Finally, write down the hidden strength/s you have just
unmasked.
*For the example above, the strengths listed might include
'big-picture thinker' and 'adaptable' (among others).*

Table 7.1 Weaknesses to strengths

1 'Weaknesses' (things I tell myself I should improve/stop doing)	2 Underlying personality trait (what is really behind this 'weakness'?)	3 Advantage environments (two situations where this trait would be an advantage)	4 Hidden strength (the strength/s this weakness was masking)

Table 7.1 *continued*

1 'Weaknesses' (things I tell myself I should improve/stop doing)	2 Underlying personality trait (what is really behind this 'weakness'?)	3 Advantage environments (two situations where this trait would be an advantage)	4 Hidden strength (the strength/s this weakness was masking)

Note: You don't have to flip all of your 'weaknesses' for this to work. If you just turn around one or two that's a strong place to start.

How to use your strengths to find your thing

When you identify your strengths, here are two ways you can use them to create a great free range career:

1. Make it yours

If five different people launched a pet-care company they would all do it in different ways: one person would round up a team and make connections with lots of people; another would write intelligently about it and sell the information online; another would form close relationships with individual pet owners; another may provide a daycare service to high-end pooches, in an environment where every detail was taken care of; another might create dog meet-ups around the world, with a festival environment and puppy-tinis for all.

Your strengths don't necessarily tell you what to do. They enable you to do whatever you want to do better than anyone else, because you'll do it your way. On your own terms. Can you add in your strengths to enhance your idea to suit you more and stand out from the norm? If there's something in your idea that you know just isn't 'you', can you take it out and replace it with a strength?

2. Create value by being yourself

Whatever you find easy and fun, someone else will consider it a chore. That means that you could build a business around a few strengths with which others struggle. However, it's more than likely that you're overlooking those strengths simply because they are so easy for you.

For example, when Rachel Papworth came to me, she had, in her words, 'become embarrassed' about her love of decluttering and organizing. However, as she worked through the free range exercises, she realized that her 'skills and passion are valuable to

2. Zoom in and take off

As Twitter co-founder Evan Williams says, 'The specialist will almost always kick the generalist's ass'. Spot something offered to a wide market and think of ways you can tailor it perfectly for a small section of that market, and in the process, snaffle up 100 per cent of that group's interest.

3. Check your back pocket

When I work with people on finding their idea, we can spend a whole session talking through options but I can almost guarantee that what they will end up doing is that little throwaway idea they mention in the last five minutes of the session. It's uncanny. The person will say that they have a 'little idea' but that it is too obvious, or maybe too crowded. Then I ask them about it, and they light up with excitement. That's when I know we're on to the winner.

Over the next few chapters you might discover some techniques that could make the impossible possible, so check your back pocket and write down anything you've been holding back.

4. Think like a free ranger

You've reached this far in the book, so in my eyes you are officially a free range fledgling. Congratulations. Just by taking on these new ideas you're already thinking differently from 90 per cent of people who stare mournfully out of the office window. So, you are no longer limited to thinking up job titles: now you can turn an idea, an interest, or even a lifelong trait – such as 'I like making people feel beautiful' – into a career.

To make this happen, *start to think of how you'd like to add value to the world*. Most people just think of a 'topic' (such as 'counselling' or 'dog training') but free rangers add in the *lifestyle* they want and *what they bring to the picture* personally.

5. Get out of your comfort zone

If you're constantly moving in the same social circles, chances are you're not encountering many new ideas. Make a point of going to ideas and creative events in your area – or even joining online courses – and meeting people who do things differently from the people you spend time with right now. What two things can you do this week that take you out of your usual habits and get you exposed to new people?

Mini case study

I spent years searching for that 'perfect' alternative career (to my role in legal marketing), hoping for inspiration but frankly getting nowhere. Then I realized that I had to get out of my comfort zone before anything would change. So I did a short course on teaching English as a second language (ESOL). That led to meeting new people, a new environment and, at last, some new ideas. I even created my own course, which I delivered to adult learners. These actions led to me moving in a new direction, with a free range 'mix' that is different from anything I would have thought of before – it's scary, it's challenging but it feels great!

Michael Devine

FREE RANGE PROFILE
Benny's story

'Travel the world, learn languages, and make a living from your website'

At the time, I was working as a translator, which was good but time consuming. I had to work long hours to come close to making enough money.

One day I was in Thailand and ran into a bunch of full-time location-independent people. They saw I was stressed out because I had to work eight hours a day while they were lying on the beach.

They suggested I stop that and start making money from my website and blog. (This was just a personal side project of me tracking my journey learning languages in three months, but over the last few months it had grown a lot of traffic.) I said no, I didn't want to put ads all over it. Instead they gave me another idea: write a guide to how to learn a language quickly, the way I had taught myself. So I did just that.

Within a month I had created the language-hacking guide, a multimedia product. It has since been translated into 24 languages. I thought at first that this $97 online guide would be a sideline, but every cent I earned for many years was from that one product.

The appeal is that I am not naturally talented with languages – I did poorly with languages at school and I'm upfront about the fact that I don't even like the process of learning! What I love is to get the learning over fast so I can speak fluently, travel and hang out with the locals. That's how a lot of people feel too. You want to be comfortable speaking socially, not stuck learning grammar for years. I show them that this can be done, from zero to chatting comfortably in three months.

To help them achieve this I write about my experiences and share videos of my progress. For example, when I went to learn Mandarin in three months, people got to watch all the way – even the bad parts! The appeal of this message, and the draw of watching my progress and my videos, means I get a lot of social media shares, traffic, and my products sell off the back of that. Now the number of hours I put in no longer has a relationship with the number of zeros in my bank account. That gives me a lot of freedom.

Benny Lewis
www.FluentIn3Months.com

08
Taking free range action

'*Do not wait to strike until the iron is hot; but make it hot by striking.*'

This chapter is a bit different: you can take a deep breath, there's no soul searching or deep thinking (phew!)

No one figures out their perfect path *just* by thinking about it. To home in on what you really want, thinking has to be backed up by a big dose of action. That's why I shared Benny's story. Benny is an action taker. When he had the idea for his blog, he had the domain name registered and the outline up within 12 hours, and was getting his first language challenge under way within 24 hours. Miles away from the six months of research that people often assume are essential before taking the first step!

Which raises an important point: what exactly should you do when you have an idea for a free range career?

The 'endless research' myth

'*I think I need to research a bit more first. If I keep reading up on the options I'm bound to stumble on the answer.*'

My client Liz was going round in circles. She would have an idea, fire up the search engine and end up spending hours at her computer, night after night, going down a research hole trapped in analysis paralysis. There were so many pros and cons, so many what ifs; the more she researched the more confused she got.

Myth buster

STOP. Do not pass the library door. Do not collect 200 websites. Online research is addictive. It gives you the illusion of moving forward, but in reality keeps you mired in analysis paralysis. There is always something more to learn. Always another 'what if?'. And at the end you still don't know what it's like on the ground. That's why no one discovers their path through doing more research.

As a bit of a bookworm I was surprised to discover that in many situations humans make better decisions with *less* information. For example, there's a study that showed that doctors make better decisions about treating back pain when they had fewer information points to go on. The ones who were given all the information they wanted, via detailed MRI scans, were misled by 'red herrings' and ended up making bad decisions.[12]

Our conscious brains simply can't handle considering large amounts of information at the same time. Plugging in too much information is like running all the applications on a computer at once: you either get fixated on one minor point, or go into overload, freeze up, and end up more confused than before.

If you can't see the woods for the trees, the answer isn't to add more trees.

Free range third way

What can you do instead of endless research? Welcome to the world of free range projects. Projects are core to free ranging – you can use them to figure out what you want, to get started and, even after you launch, you run small projects to try out new ideas without fear of failure. The typical free range business is built from a dream, followed by a series of projects taking you from here to there.

For example, Ms Cupcake, who we met in Chapter 4, began with the simple project of baking cupcakes and handing them out at the office. Then she did the same at clubs. Then she started a market stall. Then the next step and the next. *Starting in mini steps made her big dream happen.* That's much smarter (and, counter-intuitively, faster) than trying to go from 'no idea' to 'perfect bulletproof business concept' in one sitting!

There are two types of free range projects: Play Projects[13] and Test Projects. The Play Project helps you figure out if you would really love doing this idea, and the Test Project figures out if it will work in reality (and how to tweak it so that it does work). In a Play Project you look *inside* yourself and in a Test Project you look *outside* yourself. So, Ms Cupcake's first time baking in the office would have been a Play Project (to see how it felt and if it was a good fit). When she did it again – to notice people's interest in different types of cupcakes, and refine the recipes – that was a Test Project.

This chapter is your chance to start on a Play Project.

The aim of a Play Project

The aim of a Play Project is to discover whether or not you enjoy doing your idea in reality.

Importantly, this project's success is not judged by whether or not you continue with it after the first round; sometimes, the end result is that you discover that your idea wasn't quite what you expected and so you save yourself months of thinking 'what if?' (a valuable outcome in itself). For example, like Ms Cupcake, I used to have dreams of being a cake-preneur: I liked baking and was always the one showing up with a plate of baked goodies to the party. It seemed a natural idea! So, I created a little website (made by myself overnight, as you will learn, too), contacted people running local events and volunteered to cater.

The first two or three times it was brilliant fun... and then it quickly turned into a chore. I discovered that while I love baking, I don't really like having to create that many cakes so often (for such little return) – my version of fun was the process of *building the brand* and creating a positive experience, not so much having to fiddle around with frosting for six hours at a time. So, I ended up dropping that idea and building from that discovery to focus on what does work for me. *Diving in and doing the project taught me more than I learned in 18 months of dreaming and researching.* It also let me let go of the idea of being a cake-preneur, allowing my other ideas on the shortlist to fill that space. Plus, as a result of this project I met some people who ended up having an impact on the business I did go ahead with.

Play Projects can also turn into something more. The original *Free Range Humans* blog was started as my personal Play Project, and built up into something much bigger than I ever expected. The fact that you're reading this book is evidence of where a project can go!

Play Projects take the pressure off the idea that you have to decide for sure before you start something. You don't know where this will go – but start now, notice what happens and I guarantee you will discover more than you would in a month of 'thinking about it'.

Free range action

Your first project

John Williams, the author of *Screw Work, Let's Play*, is (unsurprisingly) a fan of Play Projects. Here is how he suggests you choose your first project:

1. Choose a project that excites you

Identify a free range career idea that you have been toying with. Then choose a way to get started on that in short project form. As John explains:

The aim is to produce something based on the part of this idea that is most exciting to you, be it your first portrait photo shoot or your first YouTube videos. For example, if you think you might want to be a wedding planner, volunteer to get involved in a friend's wedding; your results can be written feedback or your written summary of the event.

Remember, this is a Play Project not a 'planning project'. If you want to teach public speaking, your Play Project is *not* creating business cards or 'talking to people who do it already to see what it's like'; it is finding three people to whom you can teach public speaking and actually *doing* it. All those other parts can come later should you decide to continue.

2. Cut it down to a project that can be completed in a clear timeframe

John advises that 'your project must be one you can start and finish in 30 days maximum. Any longer and the whole thing gets overwhelming and probably you'll never start if you're uncertain already.'

I'll go a step further and suggest that if you know you tend to put things off, then make your first project something you can start and finish in *one week*.

You can extend your next project if you choose, but by choosing a shorter timeframe you a) get faster results, and b) can decide more easily (after all, this is only for the week not for life!). Your project is too big for a week, or even for 30 days? Simply cut it down to a part you can do in that timeframe. The aim is not to launch a business; it's to get started and get a feel for what it is actually like to do what you're currently just thinking about.

3. Produce something tangible at the end

Identify what you want to have to show at the end. For example, as John suggests, if you were writing that blog, your outcome could be your first three posts published. If you were running the public speaking workshop, then it could be participant feedback, or your notes for the sessions.

4. Schedule it in

Give yourself two days from today to finalize what this project will be and what you will deliver at the end. Then, mark the end date in your diary.

Hint: everyone who does this has a busy life. Don't wait for that perfect free weekend (it will never come). Instead, schedule in 30 minutes three evenings a week, set it aside as your ringfenced free range time and commit to keeping those appointments with yourself, no matter what.

5. Start

Now. And stay curious throughout: what is working for you? What do you keep putting off? Which part is resistance and which part is you screaming: 'No, this is wrong!'? Which part feels so right you didn't want to stop doing it? Take notes and build up a picture of your responses.

The aim of this is to get you feeling alive. None of this 'Oh I think I might maybe sort of like it' blandness – you want a real live 'Woah I love this and I have to keep doing it' feeling. That's an indicator of something you want to do if I ever saw one.

So, what are you going to do for your first mini project?

Mini case study

Coming across the idea of projects was a turning point. I started a pop-up cinema project that had been germinating in the back of my mind for a while. I didn't know where it would go when I ran that first film night, but when I look back I see that it changed everything.

Gradually my little 'Hey, let's put on a show, right here in the barn!' idea grew; I ended up doing it with two friends and while it started as an experiment, we've put on a film every month for the last few years. Someone gave us a screen and a DVD player, we got most of our early venues for free, and built quite a following. We did it all in our spare time. This showed me the possibility of where things can go... and I even got up the courage to resign from a job that was burning me out.

Melanie Pearson

Mini case study

I'm a planner. I plan until things are perfect, and often end up not doing anything as a result. So seeing this idea of mini projects was a gamechanger.

I decided to try out the idea of résumé writing and coaching – something I'd toyed with before but talked myself out of it. This time, I put it out there (telling people I knew and setting up a profile on a freelance site) and started doing it, alongside my day job. After the first run I refined my services based on what I learned I liked (which I only discovered by getting into motion!), got more traction, put my prices up, and soon realized I could make a go of it.

Now I use this method of free range projects all the time. In doing this I've left my job and have managed to build a free range portfolio I love including writing, editing, and running a coaching business! The 'ideal day' picture from the start of the book basically *is* my life today: I am in control of my days, my finances (and can spend more time with my family). Today I tell everyone I know who is stuck or spinning to use this approach to projects. There isn't the risk or pressure – just experiments.

Nikki Vivian

Bonus

Wondering if you're ready to do a project? Listen to this bonus conversation where I talk this through for you with my go-to person on this, Selina Barker. Selina has worked with me on free range courses for years and helped thousands of people bring their ideas to life – and find their direction in the first place – using the power of projects.

Here we talk about using this approach to help you get unstuck (be it finding your thing *or* testing a 'maybe' idea) plus behind-the-scenes stories of real people who used this to set off on their new free range career (this one is great for my fellow perfectionists): http://frh.me/projectsbonus

A word from your inner critic

'*Doing a Play Project? Listening to yourself? You don't have time for that! Stop being so selfish.*'

'*Ha ha, you still don't have a proper dream! It's pathetic: you don't know what you want at your age. Grow up.*'

'*Those are your strengths? Everyone wants to do that! Who are you to think you can get paid for that?*'

Familiar? Meet your inner critic.

Your inner critic is the voice in your head that tells you you're not good enough – it criticizes your appearance, your worthiness, your potential. It's the voice that tells you that you can't really have what you want and no one really likes you (and yes, you are too fat). It speaks to you in a way you wouldn't speak to a friend.

Author and therapist Frederick Perls describes your inner critic (which he calls your Top Dog) as usually 'righteous and authoritarian: he knows best'. As Perls explains, 'the Top Dog is a bully... he manipulates with demands and threats of catastrophe, such as, "if you don't, then – you won't be loved, you won't get to heaven, you will die", and so on.'[14]

Why are we talking about this?

Any challenge to the status quo, any attempt to actually get up and do something you love, is going to get this critical Top Dog growling. And that's probably going to happen right around... now.

If you pretend that figuring out what you want and making a change is just a tick-the-box 'rational brain' process, you're setting yourself up for a fall. *If your inner critic's fatalist words win your head space, you will give up.* He will be making an appearance on this journey, so let's deal with that.

We all have a Top Dog/inner critic. As you get closer to your 'real life', yours will get more vocal and more cutting. The question is: who's in charge? You, or that yappy voice inside your head?

Your inner critic might sound like it's speaking the truth but it is just a scared puppy (a leftover part of your ancient lizard brain) howling. So treat it gently. Here are three clues that it's your critic speaking:

- Look out for doomsday-style thinking such as, 'If you do this stupid thing you will fail and everyone will laugh at you and you will end up living in a cardboard box'.

- Take note when you speak to yourself the way you would not speak to a friend. Would you tell a friend, 'You don't have any strengths, don't be so big-headed. You're doomed to stay stuck forever'? Of course not. So why is it OK to speak that way to yourself?

- Look out for the words 'should' and 'should not' – they are your inner critic's favourite words.

What do you do when you spot your inner critic at work? Simple: realize he or she is not you. When you recognize that voice, just nod and say, 'Oh yes, that's my inner critic'. Separate this voice from your conscious thoughts and soon you'll stop seeing these doomsday thoughts as immutable fact, but as the mouthings of a scared ancient part of your brain. Some people like to give their critic a special name to reiterate it is not them.

Whatever you do don't fight against it; this puppy bites back with the most cutting words you can imagine. Your job isn't to kill it off, it's to calm it down and work around it. Remember it operates from a place of fear, so tell it it's OK, you're not going to die – you've just got one little project. Pat Top Dog on the head and send it back to sleep while you move on with your real life.

Remember, there's a big difference between the scary voice that says, 'You'll never make it!' and reality. Part of your process is learning to differentiate between the two.

*After that, the story broke on USA Today and I wound up selling
10,000 shirts on the web at $15 apiece. I cleared about $100,000.*

Rewind a moment. *The story broke* on USA Today *and he made
$100,000?* Here we were, thinking that $3,200 was a nice place to
start. How did that happen? Did Peter have secret contacts? A
qualification in T-shirt design? Peter shook his head when I asked
him, and said:

*I had no media profile, I didn't know anyone, I just made the T-shirts
because I thought it was funny and I went to Times Square and sold
them. Then, I called a USA Today lifestyle reporter and said: 'I just
did something really funny'.*

*The reporter said, 'That's hysterical. Are you selling the shirts online
now?', and I replied, 'Of course I am!' I wasn't, of course, so I had to
then run off and build the worst website in the world and, the next
thing I knew, the story ran and orders started coming in and that's
how I made my first $100,000.*

I love Peter's story for two reasons:

First, he did something *fast*. He took action before waiting to be
noticed. Most people with that idea would just talk about it with
their friends – *'hey it would be really funny if we printed that on a
T-shirt!'* – but then they would probably find a heap of reasons
why not to do it. A slightly more proactive person might get five
printed and sell them to family.

Peter took something most people would just talk about down
the pub as a 'great idea' and he made it happen without overthink-
ing – plus he shot for the top (Times Square, not your local mall!).
Crucially, he didn't get hung up on whether he had enough
experience or qualifications to make this happen. That's real free
range action.

The second reason I love this story is that even after zipping up
from 'the bottom' and selling his first T-shirts, Peter didn't settle for
the middle. After his first six hours in Times Square he turned a tidy
profit, knew he was onto something and already had a platform for

success. He could have built slowly from there and been quite comfortable. But Peter took what he had and put it on speed and went straight to the top.

Now, I am not saying that if you go to Times Square and sell T-shirts and call reporters you're guaranteed to succeed! I am showcasing this story for the attitude: Peter didn't stop at the doubts that would hold most people back. He went from idea to execution in a few days without asking for permission.

It's not about waiting to be noticed, waiting for a big break or demanding to know exactly where it will end before starting. It's not about hiding your fabulousness under the excuse *If I'm good enough they will notice me.*

It's about making things happen even while others find reasons why not to.

she had more than 100,000 fans. Today she has over 2.5 million subscribers.

Hannah's idea in its raw form was somewhat questionable. Can you imagine telling your friends: '*I have a great idea. I'm going to drink a whole bottle of red wine and cook stuff I don't have ingredients for, and then post it online and get famous! Plus I can't cook.*'

That's hardly a brilliant idea. It certainly wasn't brand new (there are dozens of other drunk cooking attempts on YouTube, pre-dating Hannah's first video. None of them had high views.). However, judging from her reviews and appearances in *Time* magazine, on *CBS News* and many other places, Hannah's execution of this idea caught people's attention. I can pretty much guarantee that had Hannah sat in a room evaluating the feasibility of this not-so-original idea then she wouldn't be where she is today.

That exposure (along with YouTube advertising revenue) allowed Hannah to quit her office job and pursue her love of making people laugh (which she's since expanded on beyond drunk cooking!).

John D Gartner, a psychiatry professor who writes on the psychology of entrepreneurs, points out that 'great entrepreneurs often do not create original ideas – they grasp the significance of an idea, wherever it comes from, and leap on it with everything they have.'[2] In other words, sometimes the best ideas sound less than promising at first and only become brilliant in the execution.

Today, you are lucky enough to be able to get an idea out into the world, for free, in a very short period of time. Use this as your platform for trying out your idea and making it original and uniquely you.

Four ways to get original (by being more you)

1. Put your stamp on it

For every person who comes up with a unique widget that goes viral, there are hundreds making a great free range living as consultants, coaches and interior designers. What matters is putting your own personal stamp on what you do.

What could you do to tweak an existing idea to be more you? This could be how you present it, how you deliver it and who you offer it to (ie could you tailor it exclusively for a specific group of people you know something about?). Instead of looking 'out there' for originality, create it yourself by putting your stamp on something that's already working.

2. Obvious to you, amazing to others

This is one for people giving advice or offering guidance.

Ever felt that everything you think of has been said before? That is a common fear. However, I bet not every idea in your favourite book was original (ie never said at any time since Plato to today). Imagine if all your favourite authors had refused to publish because *that has already been said*.

As Derek Sivers, founder of CD Baby, points out, we don't all think the same. What seems obvious to you is wildly original to someone else. He is right. I am lucky enough to hang out with some wonderful writers and thinkers, people who others hold up as examples of true originality, yet almost all of these people see their own words as nothing new. *For a fun illustration watch Sivers' short animation on originality*: http://frh.me/originalsivers

We all receive messages in different ways at different times, and most of us need to hear several people's interpretations before one hits home. So don't shy back from adding to a message you believe in. What would you say if you didn't think it was too obvious?

3. Notice connections

When Google came on to the scene it landed with a fresh approach to search. Unlike other search engines back then, its secret sauce was Larry Page and Sergey Brin's idea to rank pages in order of importance based on who mentioned them (so if a page had lots of links to it from other established websites, it would show up higher in your search).

That idea revolutionized search (which wasn't particularly good up until then!) and led to the information-at-your-fingertips world we live in today... but how original was it?

Turns out, this wasn't a 'new' idea dreamed up by technologists. It was an old idea from academia – where a scientific paper's importance is gauged on how many other scientists mention it in their own work.

Even the idea that launched one of the biggest companies in the world was not an 'innovation' created in isolation. *It was an existing idea borrowed from one field, dusted off, and used in another.*[3]

If you want to get more original, get curious. Notice what is around you, read books that others in your field don't read, get talking with people who don't work in your space, fill yourself up with inspiration and get in the habit of making connections between unrelated ideas in your everyday life. This is a killer way to create an idea that is uniquely yours.

4. Discover your difference

Want to be original? It's not just about an original idea, it's about original communication. So don't copy someone else's style: develop your own. Discover your uniqueness by getting into motion. A simple place to start is to open a free blog and write your message like no one is watching (and hey, if it's new, they probably aren't). Write twice a week and hit publish no matter what. If writing isn't your thing, do it as a simple podcast (or if you prefer in-person then run a monthly event on the topic you're interested in). However you do it, this process is one of the best ways to clarify your thoughts. You may start out sounding (or looking) like someone else, but as you show up or hit publish more and more you'll start to discover a perspective that is uniquely yours.

Above all, remember that any 'good market' will be crowded already, and if it's empty, it won't stay that way for long. You will have competition no matter what... *and that's a good thing*. It's to your benefit that someone else was the trailblazer: much easier to sell something when people actually understand what it is because other people have done the hard slog of raising awareness!

If you're really worried about competition, rest assured – using the techniques in this book (in particular Chapter 23) you'll learn how to stand out from the crowd no matter what. But for now, know that avoiding the crowd is not a long-term solution and it's definitely not a reason to back away from an idea you're attracted to.

10
Think beyond your job title

(what you have to offer other than your résumé)

'It's never too late to be who you might have been.'

GEORGE ELIOT

The 'but I don't have decades of experience' myth

'So many people are already doing this and they have decades of experience. Why would anyone pay me? Maybe I should get another degree first.'

Myth buster

If you've had ideas but felt trapped by your 'work history', you're going to love this. Outside of the career cage, no one gives you money for years of experience or qualifications. With no job interviews to pass, the résumé is no longer king, and oodles of experience is not necessarily a golden ticket to a great income.

I mean it: I have people come to me with 10 years' experience (and a master's degree in the topic) who are earning less than people with two years' experience (and a load of passion). In Part 4, you'll learn how to avoid their mistakes and stand out for real, but for now, here is a different view of what is possible with what you have.

Free range third way

Think beyond a job title

> *The first thing you should learn... is how to make yourself valuable...*
> *I succeeded as a cartoonist with negligible art talent, some basic writing skills, an ordinary sense of humour and a bit of experience in the business world. The 'Dilbert' comic is a combination of all four skills. The world has plenty of better artists, smarter writers, funnier humorists and more experienced business people. The rare part is that each of those modest skills is collected in one person. That's how value is created.*[4]

Scott Adams, creator of the 'Dilbert' comic strips

Experience is not the same as a job title. If there's something in your work or life that you a) enjoy and b) are good at, then *no matter how small it may seem right now*, you may well be able to translate it into something else of value. Combine a few of these, and that's the start of a great free range career. The first step is to identify what you have to offer with fresh eyes.

For example, Robert Watson had a corporate life that started in engineering and ended in HR. As an engineer Robert was an excellent logical thinker: 'My natural style is seeing things as a flowchart,' he explains. Then when Robert moved into HR, he learned about people's different thinking styles, and also how to communicate his direct feedback in a way that more creative types would understand. So when Robert went free range, he combined that experience and set himself up as a coach and editor for authors – a role that included being the freelance editor of the first edition of this book! He now uses his engineer-style approach –

detailed and specific – to help wordy authors (ahem) distil their message and ensure readability.

Book editing is not a 'transferable skill' you would find on Robert's résumé – he had to look at what he was good at and enjoyed (beyond a job title) to identify this hidden value. When you look beyond your traditional 'transferable skills' then you'll have something of value to offer.

If you are struggling to think of examples in your own life, consider what people come to you for help with already, and what they value about you. For example, while in his job, Robert was confused as to why people came to him – an engineer – for help with workplace conflict and life advice. So he asked, and one person replied, 'I like that you see things so logically and don't let me get bogged down in the emotions.' That was the first time Robert realized his engineering approach could be a valuable advantage in other areas.

Embrace the outsider advantage

Instead of thinking about what you don't have – or what you're 'throwing away' – consider what you *do* have. For example, Emma Reynolds went from a career in marketing to launching an HR consultancy, and said her non-traditional background was an advantage in this competitive field:

> We don't sound like everyone else – that's because we are not. That has been our biggest strength. We look at HR from a marketing perspective. The questions we ask are normal in my old field but new in HR.

> Our fresh perspective is part of why we won contracts away from the world's biggest consultancies (and were profitable from day one – even though we started out for $500 with a website I built myself). That outsider clarity has been a real advantage.

In another example, Dan Cobley, director of marketing for Google, brings unique insights to his work via his physics background.[5]

In short, when you're free range, *everything* about your life counts; nothing is thrown away. The very things that make you different might well be your edge.

Tip

When you see stories of people who are thriving in what they do, try this: instead of thinking, 'Well they fit into their field perfectly, of *course* everything works smoothly for them!' flip it around and ask, 'How were they *different* from others around them early on? What was it they could easily have hidden away but chose not to?'

Do this and you might just find the reason they rose up in the first place.

Keep in mind that your outsider edge doesn't have to be work, it can also be your personality or interests. For example, when starting out I felt different from the traditional mould of 'entrepreneur' – which is probably why I renamed it Free Range Human! My interests were different (my bookshelf is full of psychology, social anthropology and great fiction rather than mostly business books!). Plus, my personality was different (whenever I heard some guru say 'Go big or go home!' I'd think, 'Going home sounds like a great idea! I think there's tea there...').

Now, I could have interpreted that as 'I don't fit in, so should give up', and either stopped, or hidden away those sides of myself. But it's that very fascination with how we *really* work as humans, with the importance of staying oneself in a noisy world, with the power of great storytelling (basically, everything on my bookshelf!) that ended up forming the basis of everything in free range land today.

Stop comparing your inside to other people's outside

Ever been researching an idea, hit the website of someone who's already out there doing it, read their 'About' page... and immediately felt your heart sink? That person has so much more experience and status than you, how could you compete? Well here's a good first step: *stop reading other people's 'About' pages.*

The 'About' page is not an unbiased biography. It's a piece of writing created with the explicit intent of convincing the reader that the person is a perfect fit for this work. So you're unlikely to hit the website of a freelance events organizer and read:

> Laura used to work as an accountant and the only way she became an events organizer was by blagging it for the first three events, saying she organized her company's internal events – which really meant she set up last year's office Christmas party where wine was served in plastic cups (which wasn't even slightly awkward...).

> Her degree has nothing to do with her business. Actually, neither does the bulk of her professional experience. But, you know, *hire her.*

No, you're not likely to read that, even if it's true (which it possibly is). Save yourself the heartache and stop comparing your warts-and-all reality with other people's highlights reel.

Under the surface (Phil's story)

A great example of this is free range photographer Phillip Van Nostrand. Today, Phil's 'About' page looks pretty darn good – his photos have been published in the *New York Times*, he flies to weddings around the world, and is invited to photograph events such as Oscars parties in LA. He lives in a Manhattan apartment with a hammock on the deck, running multiple ventures and living an adventurous life of his design.

Lucky for him, right? Well let's go back to the start, to the day I met Phil. Back then I was a wide-eyed new free ranger on my first work-from-anywhere-with-a-laptop adventure – and the first person

I met was this curly-haired *math teacher* living in his hometown in California... with a camera and an idea. As Phil explains:

> *When I started, I wasn't qualified on paper. There was this prestigious photography school in town, but I didn't have the funds to take a year off and pay the expensive fees to attend.*
>
> *I was just a self-taught guy, without those creds on my website, and with no background in fashion or events. So I started on the side with what I did have – I honed my skills doing shoots with friends, reading up on everything I could and focusing on getting better.*
>
> *One day a friend called me and said, 'My friend is getting married and needs a photographer, can you do it?'*
>
> *'Of course I can!' I said – even though I had never done anything like that before.*
>
> *I spent the next month learning everything I could about shooting weddings, I planned everything in detail – even doing a practice shoot at the venue beforehand. I used the fee they paid to upgrade my camera equipment, got a friend with experience to come and help me out on the day – and I had shot my first wedding!*
>
> *That's how I got my first paid client. The couple loved it, and the next clients came from word of mouth and people I got to know.*
>
> *While I didn't have the usual background, I quickly learned that people bought from people that they liked and trusted, and who delivered. So I got good at those things, and put in the time to hone my craft and learn from the best at every step. I made it a point to overdeliver for my clients from the start.*

As a result of this approach Phil built up a thriving practice in his home town and became a full-time wedding photographer.

A few years later he decided to switch things up and move across the country to New York City (where he had no industry contacts) to make it as a photographer over there. Which is exactly what he has done. These days Phil is doing work he loves 'with great clients from around the world', a life designed to make the most of his new flexibility (eg visiting at least one new country a year, just to explore)... 'and no matter what, I make a point of doing things you can only do as a free ranger, like going to movies in the daytime. This is *fun*'.

Now, before you think, 'Oh well lucky for *him*'... remember how Phil felt on that day we first met, back when he was an outsider, with no contacts, gazing at what felt like a status-driven, competitive field?

What he says now is:

> *I think that not having the usual path helped because it meant I approached everything differently from the start. As a philosophy major with a teaching background I read widely – about business and life as well as photography – which meant my business was done differently as my inputs were different. I also hung out with different people, which meant I had access to different clients!*

> *Most of all I couldn't hide behind a piece of paper – so I had to think about what really mattered to clients and what I brought with my personality.*

> *The crazy thing is, these days people who graduate from places like that prestigious photo school ask to intern with me (which is great because I love mentoring!). I always tell them to keep learning, yes, but also to make the most of what you already have.*

To help you identify what you have to offer, let's delve into your Advantage Case.

Exercise: Unlock your Advantage Case

It's time to give yourself credit for what you've learned and gathered in your life to date.

In this exercise, you're writing down a 'contents list' of your Advantage Case – a virtual case packed with your hidden assets that you can take with you wherever you go on your free range journey. To give you some idea of the sorts of things that others identified in this exercise, some recent answers include:

- my ability to learn fast;
- a ready-made virtual office (that beautiful local café where I often see people work with laptops);
- being able to Google the answer to just about any question!;
- skill of finding the root cause of any problem (ie homing in on what really needs to be done);
- a supportive partner who wants me to be happy;
- skills at creating beautifully presented documents;
- my love of, and years of practice at, writing compelling stories;
- excellent organizer and planner (from years of writing and delivering lesson plans as a teacher!);
- the experience of being well travelled and good at meeting new people.

Now it's your turn. To help you unlock your hidden advantages, write down four of your own assets under each of the headings below:

Career history (think beneath the official job description and list out the parts where you feel you shine, and the things that you've loved to do):

_____

_____

Study, things you've done on the side:

_____

_____

Life experience:

_____

_____

Personal life (supportive friends, freedom, finances, etc.):

_____

_____

Personal traits and strengths:

_____

_____

Congratulations! You now have 20 advantages, and this is just the beginning. You can extend your list as you go on. Later, in Chapter 26 (Instant Status), we'll build on these to get you that positive perception that can take you from zero to must-have person in a short timeframe.

For now, remember that people thrive in any field with different backgrounds, personalities and more.

So look from another angle and start thinking free range about what you *do* have – because what the slick 'About' pages leave out is that often that's what those people who got from here to there did too.

Tip

Check yourself for Impostor Syndrome

Do you find yourself easily dismissing praise for your own advantages or successes? Do you instead focus on the reasons you're not quite good enough? If so, you might be experiencing Impostor Syndrome.

Dr Valerie Young writes about Impostor Syndrome, a mindset that means many people secretly worry about getting 'found out' for not being as smart or good as people seem to believe they are. Valerie explained to me:

If you identify with Impostor Syndrome, then it's going to be harder for you to see your own accomplishments through the same lens as you see those of others. That's because despite evidence to the contrary... you've become masterful at explaining away, minimizing, and discounting these indicators of your success with words like... It was dumb luck... The stars were aligned... oh the judges just liked me.

What you see far more clearly are the gaps in knowledge or experience, the stuff you've yet to accomplish. But it's a huge set-up. It's as if you're using a trick scale on which only negative evidence counts.

In her book *The Secret Thoughts of Successful Women* (2011), Valerie points out that people who experience Impostor Syndrome sometimes put pressure on themselves to be perfect almost immediately – an impossibly high bar. As she says: 'Remember that your first draft, first presentation, first painting, or first anything is never going to be as good as your second – or your two hundredth.'

In other words, don't use the fact that you're not world class in two hours as an excuse not to keep going.

relationship coach, speaker, virtual business manager, accountant, photographer, consultant, etc.

Verdict for full-time free range freedom

Doing something and getting paid for it is the simplest sort of business to start. When you're paid for your time all you need in order to start is to have a service to offer and be willing to offer it: there's no barrier to putting yourself out there. This means 'service'-type ideas are a great starting point for your first free range venture.

Common wisdom says that the downside of selling your time is that, well, you are time-bound. How many clients can you take on in one month? Multiply that number by your rates and that's your earning limit. However, it's not always that simple. Not only can rates be raised over time, but if you get creative with how you package and price your services you can make services earn far more, with a better and more secure lifestyle, than you may expect. Here's one way of earning more for your time:

Tip

Up your hourly rate

Supercharge your earning power by not charging per hour. Instead of saying 'I charge $100 per hour as a stylist', present your 'Style Springclean' for people who hate shopping but want to look good. You can include a fixed number of sessions, preparatory worksheets for the client, and maybe even a bonus such as recorded interviews with people who have been through this process sharing how they made sure their style changes lasted in their busy lives. You'll have an easier time selling this package for $500+ than you would selling three hours of individual consulting!

Another idea is to deliver what you do in a group setting in order to make the most of your time. For example, if, instead of

---

taking on *one* individual at a time, you work with a group of 10 people at once, you can earn 10 times as much for the same amount of time (if you keep the price the same) or 5 times more (if you halve the price compared to individual treatment). Of course, only do this if you enjoy a group environment!

However you do it, when you package up what you do and get away from an hourly rate, you escape the price-comparison game and your earnings go up. Plus it's a great opportunity to get creative with what you do.

2. Virtual products

A virtual product is one that costs you almost nothing to make and can be sold and downloaded online (eg a guide or online course). It typically contains information or motivation, and can include written words, audio, video – any medium you choose to deliver what you do to more people *without* your presence (though you're free to add in a bonus 'live' component too!).

Here's how a virtual product works: let's say you have an idea to teach public speaking to beginners. You've done this with people and find you are repeating the same advice over and over – plus you'd like to reach larger numbers of people with what you do. Solution: turn that into a virtual product.

Make a list of steps you would take people through when helping them become confident speakers. Then, jot down the parts of your teaching where most people go 'Wow, that made such a difference!' Now create the *Fearless Public Speaking* course and offer that as a downloadable product that people can do by themselves without you (*or* charge more and offer bonus support classes/a community along with it). You are now helping people and earning money independently of your time.

Of course, you can still run the live speaking training if you're excited about that, but you have the security of the virtual product helping you keep a steady income in between sessions. Your product might be an entry point leading to closer work for people who like your style after going through it, it could be part of a membership, or alternatively you could make this product your main income (like Benny did with his language-learning guide for years).

There's no one way for a product to look, and a good one doesn't have to have loads of content or information to have value. For example, if you like helping people take action, instead of holing away writing a 10,000-word guide, you might run a 'make it happen' challenge where people go from thinking about doing something to *actually* doing it. Do this online, get it right with a few first runs, and have it run smoothly time after time after that. The possibilities are endless!

Verdict for full-time free range freedom

Virtual products can give that magic balance of good earnings, flexibility and time freedom. All you require is your time, your brain, and an understanding of what your clients want, and you can create a virtual product. Make it once, and it can help people again and again (and make money over and over) no matter what you're doing.

How much can this earn? Well, common wisdom says you can't make a full-time living off a $10 e-book. And unless you have unusually high traffic, common wisdom would be right. That's why e-guides, and full online courses, cost more than $10. Do-it-yourself online courses sell from a low end of $50, and at the top end *tens of thousands*. What you can charge depends on the value you put in and how well it's tailored and presented to a specific audience.

Do the sums: if you sell an average of one a day at $100 that's around $3,000 per month. Plus, if you get creative and add in an element of interaction with you, such as a session to ask any questions and get personal help, then you can easily raise the price. Or, if you get into it, you can create several virtual offerings and the sky is the limit income-wise.

So watch out for that girl in the café tapping away at her laptop; you might think she's scraping a living with a little hobby, but she might be part of the free range generation and earning more than you imagine.

Now, I'd be doing you a disservice if I pretended that sticking up a course online will make you an instant living. You have to put in work, and it genuinely has to be good stuff that you care about. You also have to put in the time to build trust and attract people in a way that works for your personality (that's one thing I'll help you do in Part 4, so read on).

Tip

To ensure quality, make sure you've helped people with this topic in the real world before creating a virtual product. If you have the idea for public speaking training, your first port of call should not be to make an online course, your first step is to actually work with people (as discussed in Chapter 8 on Projects). Then use what you learn from that to create a meaningful product.

---

3. Advertising

Create content (eg on a website or on your favourite social media platform), bring in traffic or followers, then sell advertising or promotional space to people who want to reach those who are drawn to your content. For example, if you create a YouTube channel you can become a YouTube partner and earn from the ads they place on your page.

Examples

Emma and Ollie make their living from their YouTube channel, *My Vox Songs*, which shares their nursery rhyme animations. A world away from their former corporate jobs, their new life was made possible primarily because of revenue from the advertising YouTube places on their channel.

Dom and Rob had the idea for the *Escape the City* website while in their cubicle jobs; they started with just a free blog and ended up running an international community of 450,000 people looking for opportunities outside the traditional corporate mainstream. For the first four years Dom and Rob made their income primarily from revenue from hand-picked employers paying to post job ads to their community... even when the community was a fraction of this size! (They have since expanded the business to include online and offline programmes, but jobs ads are still part of their picture.)

Verdict for full-time free range freedom

Advertising is tempting but often misunderstood. With the exception of YouTube, signing up to a website advertising programme and whacking up ads, hoping to get paid based on traffic, will not make you anywhere near a full-time living (think of it more as coffee money). Indeed, most full-time bloggers (and many prominent podcasters) don't make their living from this sort of advertising. They tend to make the bulk of their income from virtual products sold from their website, or from consulting/services/speaking gained off the back of their thing.

The people who do well with the advertising model, such as Dom and Rob, tend to sell their own advertising space by 1) building a loyal following, and 2) doing deals with hand-picked advertising clients. Think deep rather than wide.

Free range reality check

A path that's quite visible right now is becoming a social media 'influencer' – where you grow a following on a platform like Instagram and get paid to do promotions or sponsorships. But if you've ever wondered how you're going to get millions of followers before you can do your own thing, good news: people making a full-time income like this account form a *tiny* percentage of full-time free rangers (in other words, *you have options* that do not require you to have millions or even thousands of people knowing about you!). If you're attracted to that path, but want to get moving faster, a free range approach is to build it on the side of another idea type that can get faster traction – you can see plenty of those in here!

4. Physical products

Essentially, selling real stuff – from hand-woven dog beds to art or food. You can make it yourself, commission something to be created by someone else, or even re-sell products that already exist.

Examples

A great example of the 'maker' option is Rachel Winard, who you will meet in Chapter 25. A former attorney, Rachel now makes a full-time living by selling hand-made soap in her online shop. There are also some inspiring examples of free rangers who integrate their love of travel with their business idea (such as Petra Barran who created the ChocStar van[6] and travelled across the country selling chocolate goodies at festivals and markets).

Doing products 'on the side'

Free Rangers can also do physical products on the side of another business. For example, Phil the photographer (whom you met back in Chapter 10) has, in the last few years, built up a physical products brand (La Rousse) that brings in $15,000 a month *as a side income*. What's more, it's a product he didn't even design himself:

My friend Katie showed me this beautiful glass box she had been working on – basically a glass jewellery box that photographers could put photos in when delivering to clients. She had designed it and got someone overseas to make samples. I was obsessed immediately and begged her to let me grow it with her.

We started with a simple Shopify page we built ourselves and shipped out of her garage. Creating something for a group of people we understood (photographers) really helped get it going. I gave boxes to my friends in the industry and they started to share it on their Instagram, I posted in photo communities I was in online – no advertising. We did $70,000 in sales in our first year and $180,000 the next.

When we had regular sales and started needing more stock than the garage could fit, we hired a boutique fulfilment company to do the shipping. Today we don't even touch the boxes, but it was so helpful to have done it ourselves first as we could tell them exactly what matters to the brand (right down to the pink bubble wrap!).

Phil's advice? Don't try to pre-design a *huge* range before making your first sale: start with something simple.

We started with a box in one size, and now we have a range of boxes, and more! What's funny is that our original-size box is our lowest-selling product now – you really only learn by being on the ground.

Verdict for full-time free range freedom

Physical products can be a great option but keep in mind that if you have to make as well as sell your goods (or simply buy them), then you might have to put a bit more time in to get the return you want. For this reason I usually recommend that you only choose physical products if you *know* that this is what you want to do, and are determined to put in the time to make it happen.

5. Events and experiences

These can be anything from conferences to retreats, from network-ing groups to adventures in learning and making. They can be high end (these make money primarily from the ticket price itself) or lower end (in which case the income is *usually* made either through sponsorship *or* through offering something deeper/higher value that the most engaged participants can buy).

This is particularly good for natural connectors – people who 'can't help but' bring people together.

Verdict for full-time free range freedom

If it fits you, this can be a good option for either the whole or a part of your free range picture. However, do it smartly.

Many people who take this path say that at first they mixed it with something else – especially if they were new in their field – simply as something simple like services are a great way to get to know a new field (and the people in it)... which is helpful when you're running live experiences!

Tip

If you have an idea but there are already similar-sounding events, think about what you bring to the picture. Are you fascinated with ideas? Do you like to help people relax, or do you prefer to help them make things happen? Do you want to do this for a different type of person? Whatever it is, make *that* feeling or experience the centre of what you offer

---

6. Mix it up

It's likely that a few of these approaches appeal to you. Simple solution: mix it up! This is how many free rangers create a great income and a lifestyle filled with variety.

For example, Connie Solera quit her job to run Dirty Footprints Studios, an inspiring online space and blog, where she helps people create Fearless (intuitive) art. As part of Dirty Footprints, Connie offers virtual products (such as a pre-recorded online video workshop), services and experiences (live art courses, run either as online adventures or as live desert retreats), and at one stage she included physical products (selling her own art). Each of these strands alone could have been enough to make Connie a nice full-time living, but by mixing it up Connie creates more variety and vibrancy in her day, allowing her to get paid for her loves of teaching, writing and creating art.

Mini case study

I used to be a school principal. Then, in my thirties, I quit my job and created a life and a portfolio career where I could be wherever I wanted, whenever I wanted. Now I teach an online college class, coach virtually via Skype, and recently became a Zumba instructor. I have been based in South America, Central America, Australia, South-East Asia and the Pacific Islands. I return to the Midwest in the summers and drive around, visiting friends and family.

This fall, I will attend a writing festival in Bali, interview social entrepreneurs for a book I'm writing, volunteer at a girls' school in Cambodia, catch up with friends, chase the sun and check out Myanmar.

Kristi Hemmer

Free range action

What works for you?

Gather your thoughts about the above by filling in the table below (there's room for more than one favourite in case you want to mix it up!). Write your answers below:

Table 11.1   What works for you

Model I found attractive (eg virtual products)	What I could offer (eg do-it-yourself dog-training pack)	How this fits the life I want (eg lets me reach more people and travel)	I would like to know more about (eg where to find the audience for this product)

12
How to free range-ify your idea

Now you know some ways that Free Range Humans make a living, how do your ideas fit? If your income-generating idea in its current form isn't *quite* free range enough to experiment with and get going with what you have now, help is at hand. It's time to free range-ify your idea.

The secret to free range-ifying an idea is to figure out which part of it really gets you fired up, and find another way to do that. Here's an example of someone who did just that.

Charlie Haynes started Urban Writers' Retreats in London. Currently her one-day retreats run both live and online, and she's been featured in press such as the *Guardian*. Sounds idyllic, right?

However, this wasn't the business Charlie meant to start. She wanted to create a writers' workspace, a place where members could go and work any time and host events. But she couldn't afford the rent and all of the equipment, plus having to deal with all of those overheads sounded daunting when she wasn't sure if it would work.

Charlie explains what happened next:

> *I was on my way to work one morning and had been mulling over my exercise procrastination issues. I was contemplating doing a fitness bootcamp, and it hit me that all of the things I wanted to get from the fitness bootcamp – companionship and being forced to get on with*

exercising and actually making visible progress – were the same things I wanted for myself from a writers' workspace.

I thought: if a fitness bootcamp would be better than trying to run by myself every day (and not doing it), wouldn't a writing bootcamp work the same way?

So I set up a free website and found the cheapest venue I could hire that had the minimum requirements and asked for guinea pigs, charging enough to cover the costs. I ran the event, then asked people to fill in a feedback form and make suggestions before they left, and then I made changes the next time around.

When it was clear that I could make money from this, and people got a lot done, I decided it was worth investing in web hosting and hiring a better venue. I learned how to build my website and how to do all the social media stuff, newsletters, etc. That meant it only cost a couple of hundred to get going, which I saved by not going on big nights out for a month or so while I was setting up.

Now, I run Urban Writers' Retreat days in several cities, and with the network I've built up we can do other things like residential retreats in the countryside and online courses that are simple to run from anywhere in the world.

Had Charlie sat with her original idea of a permanent writers' workspace she would possibly have never started. By the way, if you're thinking, 'She must be so brave to just dive in and get started!' Charlie would like to say:

Even without the money issue, starting was scary! Just making phone calls to potential venues was hard, but once I'd made a few steps it was easier to keep up the momentum. You can do this.

13
How to start with what you have

In this guide, I'll share the resources you need to start with what you already have – think, under $100. This is not about being tight or looking cheap. *This is about how to get champagne results on a chardonnay budget by knowing what to look for and where to get it.*

The truth is that when you look at what people spend their money on in their first year, about 20 per cent of their spending gets them 80 per cent of their results. That other 80 per cent of spending? Expensive fluff. When you know what works, and what doesn't, you can hone and get even better results without spending a fortune. Here's how I discovered this for myself.

The 100k question

A few weeks after I started on my free range venture, I was sitting in a café thinking, 'I wish someone would hand me $100,000 so I could get the word out about what I do!' I'd been thinking this a lot, and that day I realized I'd never articulated what I'd do with that hypothetical 'free money'.

So I opened up a new document and wrote out my wish list. On the list were things like 'big ads in magazines' and 'a really great website' and 'membership of high-end clubs where I can meet people doing similar things'. Then, I wrote out why I wanted each of those things.

That's when I saw it: I could have it all. How? By focusing on the *outcome* rather than the wrapping.

Table 13.1   Outcome not wrapping

What I wanted	Why I wanted it	What outcome I wanted
advertising	people would hear about me	get clients easily and consistently
website	respect and interest	get the right sort of clients easily and consistently
membership of clubs	partnerships	have fun working with others (and get clients easily and consistently)

Next, I looked at how likely it was that these wishes would get me that outcome.

Would advertising (especially advertising something that I hadn't yet had many takers for) get me enough clients 'easily and consistently'? As I knew from my previous work in marketing consultancy and analysis, the answer was 'probably not'. I figured I'd get a boost from some ads, but it wouldn't last forever.

Would a better website get me respect from potential clients and raise interest? Maybe... provided I had enough traffic (which I didn't). Would a nice website *really* convert visitors to clients? That wasn't so certain. I started to realize that the websites I was 'stalking' because I coveted their beautiful design were not websites at which I was spending real money.

OK, maybe the ideas I had for what I needed were a bit off the mark. So the question I turned to was: is spending that money the

Note: this pack is the only place in this book where we discuss business registration, tax or insurance. This is a conscious choice: I don't want to perpetuate the myth that these topics are the most time-consuming or difficult part of starting as your own boss, when in fact the opposite is true in most countries. It is almost certainly faster and simpler than you think, so don't let fear of paperwork hold you back: take action now, starting here.

Dos and don'ts of starting on a shoestring

DO make sure you have the basics: a laptop, a smartphone. Put together, both of these will cover 90 per cent of your needs; for example, I use my iPhone for photos and videos to this day.

DON'T assume you need top-of-the-range kit to get started. For example, I ran my whole business off a small, bottom-end laptop for more than a year. I set myself a goal of what I wanted to reach before buying my shiny Macbook, which made it a far more meaningful purchase.

DO get creative with free range options. For example, did you know that you can use Skype as a regular telephone? Instead of installing an extra line as a private 'work phone number', you can buy a telephone number on Skype.com. This number *looks* like a normal phone number based in your area (or wherever you choose!). When someone calls it, they are charged regular local rates and they have no idea they are calling a computer. Plus, you can call from and pick up this number no matter where you are in the world, so long as you have an internet connection.

DO have taste. Starting small should never mean looking cheap. So:

DON'T use a free business card service where the cards are a) printed on flimsy paper, or b) include the name of the printing company on the back. This says, 'I don't believe in what I do enough to spend $20 on it.' Not cool.

DON'T lose $100 to save $5. Is a saving taking up your time, mental space and stopping you moving forward? If so, that's not a saving, that's a cost.

DO invest in yourself: the best free rangers are constantly learning. That website might get re-done, but investing in your own education reaps rewards over and over.

Mini case study

Having lost my grandma, my job and my apartment over a very short period of time, I came to Indonesia to escape the questions about what I was going to do with my life. When was I going to get a job? Where would I live? I didn't have the answers – all I wanted to do was lie on the beach and process the massive changes that had happened.

I sat on the white sand, looking at the ocean and working my way through this book for the second time. I knew I wanted my business to enable me to work from anywhere and for it to be product based. But what could I sell?

I came up with the idea for my first product there, watching people taking photos of each other in the sea on their mobile phones. I thought, 'Wouldn't it be cool if your phone was waterproof?' There was my first idea. Waterproof phone cases!

I thought I'd give it a go, especially as I could see the need for it on the small island where I had set up camp for a while.

I found manufacturers online, got samples, thought of ways to improve their existing designs and worked with the factory to create my own brand: SwimCell. Taking a product that a factory already makes and putting your brand on it is called private labelling which is what I did (focusing on having great quality and making sure it looked good).

I calculated how many I would need to sell every day to cover my costs on this little island, as a mini project. It seemed doable. I spent $100 on samples then got pre-orders of 500 units from shops before committing to placing my first big order.

From the first week I've pretty much hit target. Today I pay myself a salary, have more freedom and flexibility than I dreamt of, and my business is now at a point where it runs itself even if I don't have internet access!

I was reading this book and figured, if someone else can do it, I can too.

Amy Day

14
How to know if your idea will work

(test your idea in seven days)

'You don't have to be great to start, but you have to start to be great.'

JOE SABAH

Let's recap what we've covered over the last few chapters: we've discovered that you don't need a wildly original idea, you don't need 20 years' experience, and you can get started without spending a fortune. Nice. However, a big question tends to come up right around now: *is your idea really going to work?*

Figuring out if an idea is viable isn't exactly rocket science. You need two things: 1) people who want to pay for it; 2) the potential for it to pay enough to reach the income you want.

That's what it boils down to. Are people keen to pay for it? Can you make it pay enough to suit your needs?

Let's deal with these separately, starting with the latter.

How to know if your idea can pay enough

I once received an email from someone who was trying to make a living from hand-made envelopes. She'd been making and selling her beautiful envelopes for years but never quite got it off the ground enough to cover her city lawyer salary and two mortgages. When I asked what had been holding her back, she immediately replied, 'Time. I'm so busy, but I know if I find time to make more envelopes then things will work out.'

Hmm. Something didn't add up here – and I mean that literally.

Five minutes and one calculator later it was crystal clear that in order to make her bare minimum she would have to sell more than 80 envelopes a day. That's about 2,500 a month.

When I pointed out the numbers she was floored. Somehow, this highly intelligent person had never stopped to do a five-minute calculation. Discovering the truth meant she was able to focus on making another more profitable idea work as her escape vessel, and continue to build up the envelopes on the side as a secondary income stream.

Moral of the story: calculators can be cool, kiddies. Here's how to do this for yourself right now.

Identify how much you need to make per month (very roughly). Now divide that by how much you expect to make from your main product. So if you need to make $5,000 (before tax), and your main product/service is $500 that = 10 sales per month.

That's little more than two sales a week. Now imagine you're launched, and have been out there doing this for a while, and people are interested in what you have to offer. In that scenario, does two per week (or whatever your number may be) sound like a reasonable number to achieve? If so, congratulations! You have an idea worth exploring further.

Tip: don't get bogged down in finding exact numbers. This is a sanity check, not a plan. Do the calculation now.

If you're going to go into the cookie business, Step 1 is not to plan out five years of how many chocolate chip cookies you're going to sell. Step 1 is to make a batch of cookies and see if people beyond your family will pay for it![7]

In other words, get out there and make the damn cookies.

How: 'Get it out there' does *not* mean 'quit your job and put all on the line for a crazy idea!' Instead, starting today, you can run a simple free range project. This time, your project will be a test project. It's similar to the Play Project you ran earlier in the book, but here the focus is on gauging other people's interest in what you have to offer.

Exercise: Free range action

Your first test project

In your pay test project, you get people to actually pay for something. Experimentation and real-world testing are more powerful than any focus group – it's real, and fast, and gives you outcomes you can rely on. It's one thing to say 'I'm interested' and another thing to actually put your hand in your wallet; the latter is what we get your people to do here.

Your subjects don't always have to pay with actual money (although that is ideal) but if they don't, they do have to give up their *time* or take *action* to prove their interest. Here are three ideas of ways to start your own test projects with what you have right now:

- Get two paying 'test' clients for your product or service (yes, people do this in a week).

- Run a scaled-down version of your event/course/workshop idea. Find people by putting it out among people you know, sharing in interest groups (or by creating an event on Facebook or Eventbrite and asking your friends to pass it around). Offer it for low cost in a free venue. Do charge *something* to check people are willing to pay, even if a token amount. Aim to get this going within three weeks of having the idea.

- If it's a service do the same (or think creatively!) to get your first three clients, testimonials and above all confidence as you get out there for real... without having to build a website or do big marketing. Afterwards, revise what you learned and do it at the price you really want.

What will you do for your test project?

_____

_____

_____

Once you've run your first test project, come back and consider. What worked? What didn't? Remember that your first $100 is harder to make than your first $1,000, so don't give up immediately if you get a lukewarm response. It might be because of how you're presenting it: re-jig your positioning, using the techniques in the second half of this book, and try again. Be open to your idea evolving, too. Odds are that the idea you run with will end up being a little different to the idea in your head right now. The only way to find out what works is to get out there and run it for real.

Mini case study

I was stuck in research mode... analysing my market, what to sell, would it work... the one thing I forgot was to actually create some art that I wanted to sell. Inspired by the free range approach, I finally picked up the brush and started painting. I created more than 60 pieces in six months.

I sold over 50 of my originals (plus the prints sold really well!). I started selling at local art festivals, but ended up with collectors all over the world in just one year. What I learned: staying safe doesn't get you where you want to go or any closer to your dreams. Just do something. Take action! And I did it all as a single mother with a full-time job.

Heather Dakota

Mini case study

I was getting bogged down thinking, 'I *should* build this or that kind of business', but this book took a different angle and got me creating something that focused on my strengths and what works for me. Thinking about problems I had solved for myself that I could solve for others (and that I'd enjoy doing!), I got the kernel of an idea.

I used to be incredibly sexually insecure, and knew the pain it could bring. Fearing that your partner wouldn't be happy, that they might dump you, you don't feel comfortable in yourself. I managed to solve it over a few years, but didn't find any sort of definitive resource to help. I realized that it's something that many men struggle with, and that I could help them with it too.

So I tested things out a bit, tweaked how I talked about it – and on a test project had dozens of people sign up in 24 hours! Months later I *still* get messages from people (who saw the old post I wrote about this in a forum) saying they would love to participate. From that I have success stories, saw first-hand how this has helped people, and now I am in a great position to build this up into a full business.

Paul Richardson

Where are you in your idea?

This isn't just about a good idea, it's about a good idea *for you*. When you see investors on television choose an idea to back, they can select from a wide range of ideas because what they bring to the table is their years of experience of starting and growing businesses.

When you're starting your own thing, you need to bring something personally, and as a first timer usually that contribution is going to be *understanding*. Understanding means really *getting* this area or the people. It might be having an intense awareness of this topic, moving in those circles and knowing how it feels to be in your niche's shoes. It might, more practically, be having a key skill or strength that you need in order to make this happen.

Sometimes understanding comes from direct career experience. For example, when my client Susan decided to break out on her own, she drew from her experience working in luxury goods PR to set up by herself helping luxury goods brands to build their profile and reach more people. Starting in a space similar to your experience is a simple and quick way to get going as your own boss (if you're in a hurry to get out of your job, this can be a smart move to get you started!).

Alternatively, many free rangers bring understanding based on their personal experience. For example, that's where Charlie, who you read about earlier, got going with the writing bootcamps. Her career to date had not officially been in 'writing' or 'motivating people' – but that first-hand understanding of her niche's problem got her started.

What do you bring?

Jot down some thoughts on:

- Why you got this idea in the first place (often a big clue is there).

- What's your personal experience of this area? For example, does any of your work background give you insights? Have you spent money or time learning about the area? Or, more simply, have you been through the problems your people are going through?

- Have you done any part of this in your life before? This doesn't have to be paid work, just consider whether friends come to you for help with this topic right now.

- How do your personality and natural strengths add to this idea?

- Imagine the day-to-day 'doing' of this idea. What excites you about this vision?

You don't need a hot answer for each of these questions; they're designed to get you thinking. Pay extra attention to the last two to check that yes, you are in this idea and this is really an idea that is good for you rather than good... for someone else.

Odds are that when you're really keen on an idea then you're going to be in there somewhere. If not, go back and consider: what could you change to make your idea more 'you'?

Dos and don'ts of figuring out if your idea will work

DON'T use reality TV shows such as *Dragons' Den* or Shark Tank and the hottest, sexiest new launches as your benchmark for what works. Those examples are profiled because they're unusual, not because they're the norm.

DO realize that a great idea doesn't always sound great on paper (and an idea that's great on paper isn't always great in practice).

DO remember that people don't pay for a skill or a personality trait, they pay for results. Instead of asking 'How can I get paid for this trait?' ask 'How can this trait be of value to someone else?'

DO ask yourself, 'Does this solve a problem that is bothering someone enough that they would pay to sort it out?'

DON'T assume that what someone else charges for this is your personal charging limit.

DO the $100 test:[8] make it a rule that if you like an idea, you stick with it until you earn your first $100. Then you can revise it.

This approach takes the pressure off thinking it has to be a 'forever' commitment and lets you find out a lot about the idea as you reach that goal. Also, you get $100.

DO think smart. If you know people are making a living from your idea, then there's no need to reinvent that wheel; their existence proves customers are paying. Instead focus on discovering where *you* are in this idea and making sure it's solving a problem people care about. Think like a free ranger and adapt these exercises to your situation; there's always a gap in the market for people who think smart.

FREE RANGE PROFILE
Susan's story

From idea to income in 10 weeks

Susan Sjölund had a high-flying career doing in-house PR for an interior designer, yet while she enjoyed the glitz and the glam of that world, she knew she wanted something more. Frankly, she was sick of the packed commutes and spending her summers trapped in the office:

> I remember those days in the office... the ones when I would rather stick a fork in my eye than churn out another report or have to think up another excuse for why I'm 10 minutes late on a day where I had nothing pressing to do anyway.

Then, Susan moved from New York to London, and took this opportunity to change her work life as well as her location. Susan knew the lifestyle she wanted. She no longer wanted to work for someone else; she wanted to be in charge of where, when and how she worked.

But there was a snag: Susan had no idea what she wanted to *do*. All she knew was that whatever she chose had to generate an income that would allow her to purchase that Burberry jacket she'd fallen in love with the week I met her for coffee in Soho: 'I still have to be able to buy beautiful things!' she said, 'That's not something I can give up.' (This might be the first jacket-inspired life change.)

To figure things out, Susan signed up to my coaching programme, and after the first week I was hit by the realization that I'd just met someone who is a wonderful bundle of energy who *makes things happen*.

In less than 10 weeks Susan had:

- figured out what she wanted to do;
- launched her new business;
- landed her first major client... the designer Nicky Haslam (the girl aims high!).

To get started fast in her new free range life, all Susan needed was a website, which she created herself in WordPress. She got a friend to design a logo, wrote the copy herself and asked clients for images of their work. From there things grew fast: Susan emailed me to share that she had billed her clients about $50,000 in the first six months and things just went from there.[9]

Q&A with Free Range Susan

What was the moment you figured out what you wanted to do?
The best thing I did was the exercise where you match up things you love with what you have to offer – that was the 'lightbulb' moment for me! Once I figured that out things started to fall into place.

Did you end up buying that jacket?
Yes! There was also the day where I bought myself *three* Jimmy Choo handbags. The oily green one with the snakeskin handles paid for the entire experience when Nicky noticed it straight away on our first meeting and said, 'What a great bag'. A girl's gotta do what a girl's gotta do!

What's your advice for people reading this book?
Don't downplay the scariness of it. It is s**t scary. Particularly if you're going it alone. But if you believe that there is a market for your product or service, the only way you'll know whether it will work or not is to go for it. If you don't, that nagging little voice in the back of your head will forever be telling you, 'What if...?'.

Susan isn't a magician. She didn't stumble across opportunities by luck. She was just smart, self-aware and determined to put in the time and energy to make a real change.

Part Three reflections – your starting point

Now it's time to pull together your thoughts from this section.

This is the space to capture the idea or two that you're most keen to move forward with. So: what free range career idea is most attractive to you right now?

_____

I want to start my free range career by offering (give a summary of your idea):

_____

This will give me the freedom to:

_____

(for example, get paid to do what I love/have, more time/work, where I choose, etc)

_____

On the scale of 1–10 of how much this possibility will rock my life I give it a:

_____

What tip could you use from the Original Idea chapter (Chapter 9) to make your free range offering more unique?

_____

What did you find in your Advantage Case? (Chapter 10)

_____

Which free range business types were most attractive to you? (Chapter 11)

_____

What were your favourite resources in the 'Start for Under $100' pack? (Chapter 13)

_____

What did you learn from Pay Test 1: the problem-solving exercise? (Chapter 14)

_____

What you are going to do for Pay Test 2: your first test project? (Chapter 14)

_____

Note: if you're uncertain which free range career you want to take forward, don't stop! Simply write down whatever you have (or whatever seems most attractive) right now. You can always come back and change your answers as you discover more by taking action (ahem) and using the resources in this book. Do this, then read on.

CONGRATULATIONS! You reached the end of Part 3. Now we move to the next step, looking at how free rangers go from an idea to full-time income (in a way that lets their personality shine and their lifestyle dreams become reality).

But before then, it's time for my personal favourite part of this book: 'The Interlude'. Turn the page and take a look.

Notes

1 Ciarallo, J (2010) Vocus acquires Help a Reporter Out (HARO), Adweek, 10 June, https://www.adweek.com/digital/vocus-acquires-help-a-reporter-out-haro

2 Gartner, John D (2011) *The Hypomanic Edge: The link between (a little) craziness and (a lot of) success in America*, Simon & Schuster, New York

3 Brin, S and Page, L (1998) The anatomy of a large-scale hypertextual web search engine, http://infolab.stanford.edu/~backrub/google.html;

Mejia, Z (2018) 8 facts you might not know about Google's early days, CNBC, 4 September, https://www.cnbc.com/2018/09/04/8-surprising-facts-you-might-not-know-about-googles-early-days.html

4   Adams, Scott (2011) How to get a real education, *The Wall Street Journal*, 9 April http://online.wsj.com/article/SB10001424052748704101604576247143383496656.html

5   http://www.ted.com/speakers/dan_cobley.html

6   After years of adventures in the ChocStar van Petra launched a different free range project: KERB (which became a huge street food movement in London). She now lives in New Orleans, on her next adventure. You never know where things will go!

7   As quoted in Sanders, I and Sloly, D (2011) *Zoom: The faster way to make your business idea happen*, Financial Times/Prentice Hall, London

8   Thanks to Barbara Winter and her '$100 hour' idea for inspiring this tip!

9   After several years running this particular business and thriving with it, Susan expanded into exciting new projects including joining forces with some new startups working on causes she was passionate about, moving countries (twice – the second time with her husband and new twins!), and more – all to say that you never know where your first free range career steps may take you!

Interlude
Free range reality check

As you start on this journey, you're bound to hear people tell you to 'be realistic' about your options. Those voices can be quite off-putting, so I wanted to show you another perspective before we move on to how to make your new life happen. The next four chapters have no exercises or actions... just a rush of reasons why yes, this is possible, and why a negative voice is not necessarily a reason to give up. Grab a cup of tea, sit back and enjoy a free range reality check.

15

Meet the people who don't want you to escape the career cage

(or: the beige army unmasked)

'Keep away from people who try to belittle your ambitions. Small people always do that, but the really great make you feel that you, too, can become great.'

MARK TWAIN

This chapter's message is really important but it's one that some people (some people who you and I both know) won't want you to read.

These people, the ones we both know, are a type that you come across every day (shh, there's one in the office with you now!). They prefer tradition and routine to innovation and enthusiasm, and think that your dream of a freer, more fulfilled life is a dangerous fantasy best quashed soon.

They are the beige army, and they have more of an impact on your life than you realize.

The beige army are the managers in the office who can't see the big picture – they prefer to nit-pick on the 1 per cent negative instead: 'Yes, well done for launching that project that might change the world, but you didn't fill in this line in form 30B in triplicate.'

The beige army are staid, repressed and terrified of change, but that's not why I have a problem with them. After all, it's up to them how they live their lives. I have a problem because they want *you* to be that way too.

They wander around the corridors of your office block (and, perhaps, your extended family reunions) judging anyone who does anything outside of *their* comfort zone.

Should you be so audacious as to consider an option (for yourself) that the beige army finds challenging to *their* beliefs, they purse their lips and say, 'Are you sure that's wise?' They furrow their brows and ask, 'Why would you want to do that? Why don't you just get another job?'

Ever heard that? Then you know that it's not a question, it's a statement. What they really mean is:

> *If you do that strange thing you will crash and burn and fail and you will be laughed at. No one will be on your side and you'll end up in the gutter, miserable, harkening back to the golden days when you were safe here, safe with us in this beige existence where nothing changes, ever.*

That's what the beige army wants you to think whenever you consider making a change outside of *their* comfort zone. Venture to voice a different perspective and, certain of their world view, they'll curl their lips with a little smug sneer and say 'yes, alright darling'. And almost certainly ignore you.

The truth is the beige army is just a group of scared but vocal people

All of us get scared about our lives:

- Are we the person we imagined we'd be?
- What if this is all there is to life after all?
- What if we get it wrong? What if we get it right?
- What if it turns out we are not good enough after all?

These are big scary questions.

If you've asked yourself any of those questions – felt the fear and admitted to yourself that you were scared – then you're not a member of the beige army. All of us get scared, that's part of being human; what's really evil is that the beige army won't own up to their fear.

The person in the beige army doesn't look like a terrified animal, but they are. Their criticisms of others are their weapon against facing up to their feelings. They're living a lie: they pretend they're doing the 'right' thing (in fact, they pretend this so much that they no longer remember they are pretending). All they know is that if one of those 'other' people who are 'different' from them come on their turf, they get het up. Any alternative is far too scary for them to contemplate.

Everything the beige army says is a manifestation of their fear. For example:

- **They question your worthiness**: the beige army hears about your idea for a blog and says, 'How can you write on that when you don't have a PhD in the topic?' or 'Are you sure it's wise to start without a reputation?'
  They don't dare to do anything without 'qualifications' and permission, because they have never believed in themselves (so why should you?).

- **They criticize from the outside without putting themselves on the line**: the beige army are the (anonymous) online critics who harshly rip into 20 books on starting a business, but never get the guts to start a business themselves; the people who look at your project and criticize details without daring to start their own thing.
  They don't dare because they think that people will be as harsh and critical of them as they are of other people.

- **They make you feel small and naïve**: the beige army are the people who hear your plan, put on thin smiles and say, 'Meanwhile back on planet earth'. Or they'll snort and say, 'Good luck with that'.

They make you feel small, because believing that any other possibility exists calls into question their life choices; they can't stand feeling vulnerable.

Ever heard from someone like that and questioned yourself as a result? You're not alone. I've seen people on the edge of making changes give up because of someone else's fears.

Yet thinking and acting in this way has got the beige person to where they are now. So ask yourself: do you want to be in their shoes? Do you want their job, their attitude and their life? If so, take their advice, because that's the way to get there.

The beige army's biggest weapon is its pretence that it represents everyone

In their worldview, everyone has a job:

Do you want to throw away your career and be a weird broke hippie? Everyone knows that it's a bad, hard world out there: the most sensible thing to do is stay safe, keep your head down.

Everyone knows that.

Of course, everyone doesn't think like this. But as the beige army is so vocal and certain, you'd be forgiven for thinking otherwise. It's hard to do something against what 'most people do': most of us don't want to be 'odd' or 'not quite normal', do we? That human desire for acceptance and inclusion is what the beige army banks on to keep you in line.

But the beige army *are not the normal ones*. They're the sad, repressed folk who live their lives barely feeling anything anymore. They've turned off their emotions inside and they want you to do that too. They're not the majority... they're just *loud*.

So let's call them out for what they are. The people who say, 'It's not possible', 'That's a bit weird', or 'Why don't you just get a different job?' do not speak for society and they do not speak for you. They are just a group – the beige army – and they're dead scared of getting any bright, lively paints on their bland beige uniform.

How to overcome the beige army (your battle plan)

Once you've named them for what they are (the 'beige army', not 'everyone'), there are three things you can do to stop them from stopping *you* moving forward:

1. Know you are not one of them

The beige army is a big group, mostly because they are so good at influencing others by making them feel small if they act differently. It's easy to be taken in by their certainty, and even adopt their characteristics.

Here's the difference – if you act like a beige soldier, you'll hate yourself a little for it ('oh my god, I've become a bureaucrat!'), whereas they pride themselves on being mundane. Whenever you recognize that in yourself, a moment of difference in attitude, hold on to it, because daring to be different is your shield from their attacks.

2. Be human

Be enthusiastic and surround yourself with folk who are free range thinkers. Displays of passion – be it talking enthusiastically or showing emotion – are terrifying to the beige army. They will laugh at it and belittle it: 'Alright, tone it down there', 'Hmm, getting a bit carried away?'

However, Brené Brown, a research professor who spent her career researching vulnerability, courage and shame with thousands of people, points out:

> *You cannot selectively numb emotion. You can't say, 'Here's vulnerability, here's shame, here's disappointment: I don't want to feel them so here's a beer and a banana nut muffin.' You can't numb those*

hard feelings without numbing the other emotions. When we numb hard feelings, we numb joy, we numb gratitude, we numb happiness. And then we are miserable and we are looking for purpose and meaning.[1]

So don't listen to the beige army call to keep mum and keep numb. Instead, find your true tribe and spend time with them. Immerse yourself in their writing, their events, their experiences; share their passion and soon you'll stop seeing the beige army as the 'normal' ones but as strange creatures to be pitied.

3. Use your secret weapon

Here's the biggest thing you can do to fight them: don't. The beige army are impenetrable people who – in the name of avoiding discomfort – have numbed themselves from feeling.

A beige person is like a rock: nothing moves them, so don't bother trying. There's no point trying to convert them. Just walk around them. (Then, when you end up doing well, they'll change tack and pretend they were on your side all the way.)

I'm taking on the beige army, but I'm not interested in beating them. This isn't about winning an ideological argument with a group of terrified people. It's about getting around the big, critical, scared blob of a barrier in your way so that you can live your own life.

Once you're on the other side you'll look back and wonder why they ever had any power over you. You'll smile, turn your back on their fear, and walk forward into your real life in full colour.

16

What to do with those Reasons Why Not

'Argue for your limitations and, sure enough, they're yours.'

RICHARD BACH

The 'not for the likes of me' myth

'Sure, these stories are nice but there are a lot of reasons why I can't do this. They had an advantage that I don't have – it's nice to dream but my situation is different; I have so many Reasons Why Not.'

Myth buster

In writing this book, I've spoken to some of my favourite free rangers who broke out of their careers to go and create lives most people dream of. At the same time, I've also been speaking more and more to the people who desperately want to do the same, but feel stuck.

The single thing that separates the ones who have broken out from the ones who haven't is stupidly simple. It's not money. It's not age. It's not some smart strategy they are yet to hear.

It's their attitude to the Reasons Why Not.

I actually want to slap myself down for saying that. How clichéd is that? Have the right attitude and you'll succeed?! What a load of rubbish. Except for the part where it's true. *Darn that reality.*

I have spoken with Free Range Humans of all backgrounds: people with kids or without. Graduates from the top schools in the world and university dropouts. Careers spanning every industry you can imagine.

On paper, these people are wildly different from one another. But when it came to handling the Reasons Why Not you could map their words over each other:

> *Melissa Morgan: 'Not knowing enough is not a reason why you can't do this. I knew nothing about business when I started. I learned everything by myself. In today's world no one can honestly say they can't find information.'*

> *Benny Lewis: 'Any excuse you can come up with, someone has gotten around it. You could have no natural talent, it doesn't matter – a lot of idiots do great things. You could be as poor as you can imagine – people do it. I tell people to look at the likes of Helen Keller who was a blind and deaf woman in the 19th century yet wrote books, spoke multiple languages, met two American presidents – imagine what she had to overcome, and tell me how you can come up with excuses why you can't do something?'*

> *Peter Shankman: 'There's always going to be a reason why you can't do this. We all have bills to pay. Find ways around the barriers.'*

Why is this so important? Because the inverse is debilitating. Corbett Barr, online entrepreneur and podcaster, explains:

> *There are people who look for* unfair advantages *when they hear about someone's success story. They like to point out connections, money, special talents and other reasons why success was possible [and] why they couldn't do the same thing.*

Looking for 'gotcha' advantages in other people's stories misses the point. Naysayers ignore the perseverance and incredible effort the hero in question had to bring to the table. They ignore the obstacles overcome on the journey.

Whether you habitually attempt to discredit others' successes might tell you something about your own chances of success.[2]

Why should someone else's advantages be your limitations?

Free range third way

Instead of focusing on what you don't have, do what every Free Range Human does and focus on maximizing what you do have (if you struggle here, go back to the Advantage Case exercise in Chapter 10).

Also, get into the habit of picking your similarities to – rather than differences from – the people in success stories. For example, pick a success story that you find attractive. What similarities do you have to that person? No 'buts', just list the similarities.

Now, imagine that same person before they made a change. What excuses could they have used that the change was not possible? Remember: they didn't know it would work when they started, so what reasons could they have found to prove that they were at a disadvantage?

Then, get aware that when you *do* do that Impossible Thing That You Just Can't Do Right Now, people will pick at least one item off your advantage list above, and they will say, 'Oh, *of course* they made it happen, they had *that* thing so it was all easy for them'.

After you pick your jaw off the floor, you'll know that wasn't true. You'll know you still overcame obstacles and worked hard for it. Exactly like every other person who has done something out of the ordinary.

No matter how many how-tos we learn, there will always be a Reason Why Not. How you handle your Reasons Why Not is the greatest indicator of where you will be this time next year.

Dos and don'ts of starting (at your age)

DON'T believe that inner voice that tells you you're 'too old' (or 'too young') to do this. The truth is that people at *every* age think they are either too young or too old. There is no perfect age: only now.

DO realize you can use your age to your advantage. For example, if you're older than average you'll come across as more experienced even if you're new to a field, so use that. If you're younger, people tend to assume you have a fresh and sharp perspective – feel free to play on that.

DON'T expect other people to accept you until you accept yourself. The biggest barrier with age (in the free range world) is when you're uncomfortable with it and haven't put in place strategies to make it work for you. Get yourself comfortable with your age for other people's perceptions to follow.

DO remember the words of Julia Cameron in *The Artist's Way*: 'Do you know how old you will be by the time you learn to play the piano? The same age you will be if you don't.'

Mini case study

In my forties I decided I wanted a change from the nine-to-five office drudge. So one morning on my way to work I saw a guy working in our local park and thought, that looks good, I'll do that.

Long story short – it took me eight months of hassling the local council to hire me and eventually they gave me a job (hoping it would kill me, I think). I was located with a hot-mix (bitumen) gang and my job was to dig up the patches of road that needed repairing, then throw it on the back of the truck, and then shovel the hot mix into it. Very hard work physically. I was only 8 stone. At the end of the day I could just make it home, eat and go to bed. Women didn't do that kind of work in those days so I was also a bit of a trailblazer.

But I *loved* it, and got so fit, and after a year or so I decided to be a fitness instructor, so I got qualified and worked my own hours in gyms, which then led me to being interested in people and how they operate, which led me to life coaching, which is what I do now.

I am now in my sixties, which I know sounds ancient but believe me that is just a crock. Another excuse to give up. I am an avid cyclist and runner and have a fantastic relationship of 25 years. We travel and work around Australia, doing what we love and having fun. I recently acquired my NLP Practitioner qualification and just love learning, and want other people to realize they can pretty much do anything, regardless of age.

Joan Bell, Australia

Now I know I had been living with depression and anxiety for a long time. I can't think of a single corner of my life they haven't touched, even before I knew what it was. And none more so than in my work.

Not only did this lead me to step out of that career-cage world in the first place, it also informed how things came together.

You see, I didn't quit my job with a grand intention to 'dominate the world'. I quit my job to create a life and an income in a way that would work for who I was.

But this was different to what the 'business books' I was reading were talking about.

So I asked myself: how could I create a custom career *and* a really-me lifestyle and income from the ground up? Long story short – that's the origin of the free range movement you're reading about in this book.

Here's what that means for you.

Free range thinking (under the surface)

Whether or not you found the above familiar, what *every* successful free ranger has done is designed their idea to accommodate their personality or unique circumstances. They didn't contort themselves to fit into someone else's box.

But the catch is, you rarely see it from the outside.

From the outside it can look like every field, every idea, every business type has a certain way that you 'should' do it. I can't count how many times I've heard someone say, 'Well if that's the way *that* big-name person does things, I have to do it that way too'. But consider this: what if that other person's method was actually a workaround? Something they came up with to work for their circumstances, or their personality?

Here's an example.

These days I have a policy of never running something alone. Partly because I like bouncing ideas off people – but *mostly* it started out because I wanted to be sure I was covered on all fronts on the off-chance my head wasn't in the game for a few days. Yet that workaround soon became part of my 'edge'. I quickly learned how to draw on other people's strengths, to pick the best like-minded experts to work with me – so my clients ended up getting *more* value and our work got even better! What's more, my work spread more because of those collaborations too.

To be clear, a solo person, always collaborating, was not the normal 'blueprint' when I started! But here's the thing. Since then I've had several people say, 'Oh I'd like to do something like you... but I don't love collaborating like you do!' – without realizing they were looking at my *personal workaround*, and making that a *requirement* to them doing an idea.

So when you see people do things in a way that just isn't *you* – pause for a moment. You might have thought you were looking at 'the way things have to be for a business like that', but consider that you may be looking at someone's workaround...

And if that person has a high enough profile, soon that way of doing things might seem like the norm.

That does not mean it has to be the norm for you.

Free Range is not some one-size-fits-all formula

Today my free range life has many custom workarounds you may not guess from the outside: where I work day to day, how my year looks.

For example, I created my first online course *not* because it was what some anonymous guru said to do, but because it was a way of 'bottling' me at my best, to be able to reach people at the times I was not. See, I know that my biggest asset – my brain and being – can be strongly on, but also strongly off. At times I think with extremely fast, razor-sharp clarity – at other times the fog comes down (I also have times I am deeply into one part of a topic, and times I am deeply into another). Rather than berate myself for it or pretend that stuff isn't real, I got realistic and tweaked things to work with it.

Had I followed the crowd, I would not be doing my free range thing.

The moral is this. You don't have to copy someone else. You may be looking at their workarounds and unwittingly deciding that you can't possibly do the same. Your energy is best spent making design choices that suit your circumstances.

This story is mine, but it isn't mine alone. So often there's more to the picture than the shiny story you see at first glance. Most importantly, they are successful free range careers that the people created on *their terms*.

For example, today Jo Gifford runs a thriving online business, with marketing and branding programmes that are making waves around the world. A breath of fresh air in what is usually a formulaic field, Jo is bright, funny, intelligent, and gets great results. 'Shiny-haired and confident', right?

Well scratch the surface and you'll find that she lives with *three* chronic illnesses (and two young children) and runs most of this from her couch (as that's what her body needs in order to function). Jo explains:

I'm a lifelong achiever. I wanted to just get on with things, so I spent a long time trying to push all that down and out of sight. I kept trying to fit myself into how you were 'supposed' to do things – like schmoozing clients and being on call. Then I hit a wall and realized I couldn't grow something any further without being realistic about who I was.

That's when I came across this book – I inhaled it in an afternoon, and just kept thinking, 'Of course, of course you can design something to fit you'. The more I looked at the free range world, the more I thought, 'Heck yes – I could do things my way!'

So Jo rewired who she worked with, started a new brand with a fresh way of working, and is now doing better than before – with a unique structure of working that fits who she is:

I manage my health and family commitments with much more flexibility and success, I have increased my income and been able to do passion projects alongside my work – essentially, I am thriving outside the box.

Mini case study

I'm a real introvert, and need a lot of space to be at my best. Talking on the phone or being in meetings all day throws me. I could pretend that wasn't true, but it is me.

So I got real and set things up on my terms. I created 'working conditions' where I am clear about my hours and the way I work with clients. My days start at 10 am; email checking around 3 pm. Any calls are after 3 pm if at all – that's when I get social. I never do client work on Wednesdays – that's my day!

Someone once said to me, 'If you make yourself that unavailable, you won't have any clients!' Well, guess what? I'm 10 years in and that isn't true. I have great relationships with my clients because I've set up a way of working that lets me be at my best for what I do with them.

Jenn Hume
www.hellyeahtech.com

These under-the-surface stories are everywhere when you start to look. Remember Peter Shankman? He attributes much of his business success (across all his ventures) to ADHD: the very thing that has also been his greatest Achilles' heel.

For others it's less mental or physical health and more about difficult life circumstances. Or simply a personality trait.

So while people in stories might sound confident, and while that confidence is often real in that moment – remember, it's not always the whole picture. This isn't about *perfect people* doing *perfect things*... it's about real humans doing what they can with what they have. There will be breakups and families, breakdowns and highs, global events and loss, and still amid all that – we do the work.

Why am I talking about this here, halfway through the book? Because this matters. Because without unpicking these stories it's hard to see the human side, especially how much engineering has gone into *moulding* ideas to suit the people you read about. And it's by seeing the human side for others that we can start to craft a more human and more right free range career for ourselves.

So the message is: *don't look for someone else's blueprint*. Design your own to suit your particular circumstances. Tweak it as you go, as necessary, but keep it always yours.

Above all, don't go down the old way of thinking, where an idea or business tells you who you should be – from here on in you are a free range human, and it's the other way around.

> Did any of this get you thinking about ideas that you might have overlooked because of how you see other people doing them? Or even about how you might make an idea even more 'you'? As these thoughts come to you, go back to the last exercise (at the end of Part 3) and tweak your answers as needed!

FREE RANGE PROFILE
Jon's story

How to quit your job, move to paradise and get paid to change the world

One more story for you before we move onto the practical side of Part 4!

This is a guest chapter by Jon Morrow, full-time blogger and Free Range Human. He has a story I think you need to hear. Whatever you had planned for the next few minutes put it down and read this. Really.

Jon's story

It's fun to dream about your blog or business idea taking off and changing your life, but sometimes you wonder if it's just that: a dream. In the real world, dreams don't ever come true.

Right?

Well, let me tell you a little story...

This is how I quit my job

In April 2006, I was hit by a car going 85 miles per hour.

I didn't see him coming, and I don't remember much about the accident, but I do remember being pulled out of my minivan with my shirt on fire. The front end of the van was torn off, gasoline was everywhere, and my legs were broken in 14 places.

For the next three months, I had nothing to do but endure the pain and think about my life. I thought about my childhood. I thought about my dreams. I thought about my career.

And overall, I decided I didn't like the way things were going.

So I quit.

Hearing about my insanity, a friend called and asked me, 'Well, what are you going to do now?'

'I don't know,' I told him. 'Maybe start a blog.'

And so that's what I did.

For the next three months I didn't just tinker around with blogging, I dedicated myself to it. I started work at 8 in the morning and I kept going until 11 at night. I didn't watch television. I didn't see my friends. From morning till night I was writing, reading and connecting with other bloggers. Nothing else.

Within two months it was getting 2,000 visitors a day and was nominated for best business/money blog of the year. A couple of months after that, Brian Clark asked me to become the Associate Editor of Copyblogger, and so I sold up for five figures and went to work at one of the most popular blogs in the world.

And, amazingly, that's just the beginning of the story.

How I moved to paradise

Have you ever woken up one day and realized you secretly despise everything about where you live? The weather is horrible. Your neighbours are jerks. You don't like inviting anyone to your home because it's always a wreck and you're ashamed of how it looks.

Well, that's exactly what happened to me. In January I was sitting in my pathetic apartment, wrapped up in blankets to keep warm, trying to get some work done on the computer, when it struck me how monumentally stupid it was.

I was a full-time blogger, for God's sakes. I could do my work from anywhere in the world. Why on Earth was I living in this hellhole?

The only problem was I had no idea where I wanted to go, but a couple of weeks later the telephone rang and it was a friend who had retired to Mazatlán, Mexico. As usual, he was calling to gloat about the weather and the food, but instead of just suffering through it this time, I stopped him and said, 'No, don't tell me any more. I'm moving there.'

'What? When?' he stammered.

'I don't know exactly when,' I told him, 'but I'm starting right now.'

Two months later, I took a one-week trip to scout it out and look for places to live. When I got back, I started selling all of my stuff, packing the rest of it into storage, and saying goodbye to friends.

Almost one year to the day after our phone call, I hopped in the car and drove just shy of 3,000 miles to my new beachfront condo in the finest resort in Mazatlán.

As I write this, I'm sitting on my balcony with my laptop, watching (no kidding) dolphins jumping out in the Pacific. It's a sunny day, there's a nice breeze, and I'm thinking about ordering a piña colada from the restaurant downstairs.

Lucky me, right?

Well, what might surprise you is I left out a piece of the story. It's the part where I have a fatal disease. I can't move from the neck down, and yet I essentially get paid to help people.

Let's talk about that part next.

How I get paid to change the world

You know what's funny?

The worst part about having SMA [spinal muscular atrophy] isn't how everyone treats you like a charity case. It's not the frustration, anger or depression.

No, the worst part is the freakin' *bills*. The doctors. The medication. The nurses.

I added it all up and the total cost of keeping me alive in the United States was $127,000 a year. That's not rent. That's not food. That's *just* medical expenses.

Granted, I didn't actually have to pay all that. I had private insurance, Medicaid, other government aid programmes, but all that support comes at a price: they control you. The government allotted me only $700 a month to live on, and I had to spend every single cent above that on medical expenses, or they would cut me off.

So for years, that's what I did. If I made $5,000 one month, I set aside $700 for living expenses, and I spent the other $4,300 on medical bills. Nothing was left. Ever.

And eventually, I got sick of it.

I wanted to make money without having to worry about losing my healthcare. I wanted to take care of my family instead of them always having to take care of me. I wanted to actually live somewhere *nice*, not some ratty little apartment built for folks below the poverty line.

The only problem was it just wasn't possible for me in the United States.

No matter how I played with the numbers, I couldn't make it work. So, I did something crazy: I quit Medicaid. I moved to Mexico. I stopped worrying about myself at all and started a business based on one simple idea: helping people.

I found up-and-coming writers who wanted a mentor, and I trained them. I found businesses who wanted to cash in on social media, and I developed their strategy.

In exchange, they paid me what they could. Some folks gave me $50 an hour and others $300 an hour, but I treated them all the same and I dedicated myself to making *their* dreams a reality.

The results?

Within two months, I was making so much money so fast that PayPal shut down my account under suspicion of fraudulent activity. Today, not only am I making more than enough to take care of myself, but a couple of months ago I got uppity and bought my father a car.

Do you understand how precious that is? For a guy who can't move from the neck down to buy his father a car?

And the best part is, I'm not making money doing mindless drudgery. I'm *changing people's lives*.

Every day, I get emails from readers who say my posts have changed their thinking. Every day, I get emails from students who say my advice has changed their writing. Every day, I get emails from clients who say my strategies have changed the way they do business.

I can't really believe it. Normally, a guy like me would be wasting away in a nursing home somewhere, watching television and waiting to die, but here I am speaking into a microphone and essentially getting paid to change the world. If my fingers worked, I'd pinch myself.

And here's the thing: I don't want it for just me. I want it for you too.

The reason I told you this whole story wasn't just to brag but also to convince you of one incontrovertible point:

You can do this!

You want to quit your job and become a professional blogger?
   You can.
You want to travel around the world, living life to its fullest?
   You can.
You want to dedicate your every hour to helping people and making the world a better place?
   You can.
Because listen... I know it's horribly cliché, but if I can quit my job, risk the government carting me off to a nursing home because I can't afford my own healthcare, convince my poor mother to abandon her career and drive my crippled butt 3,000 miles to a foreign country, and then make enough money to support myself, my mother, my father, and an entire nursing staff using nothing but my voice then what can you accomplish if you really set your mind to it?
   My guess: pretty much anything.

No, it won't be easy. At some point, I *guarantee* you'll want to quit. I *guarantee* people will treat you like you're insane. I *guarantee* you'll cry yourself to sleep, wondering if you made a horrible mistake.

But never stop believing in yourself. The world is full of naysayers, all of them eager to shout you down at the slightest indication you might transcend mediocrity, but the greatest sin you can commit is to allow yourself to become one of them. Our job isn't to join that group but to silence it, to accomplish things so great and unimaginable that its members are too awed to speak.

You can do it.

I believe in you.

So get started.

Right freaking now.

This article originally appeared in longer form on www.problogger.com.¹ *Many thanks to Darren Rowse of Problogger and Jon Morrow for permission to share it here.*

Notes

1 Brené Brown: The power of vulnerability https://www.ted.com/talks/brene_brown_on_vulnerability
2 Corbett Barr, Do You Turn Advantages into Limitations? http://www.corbettbarr.com/advantages-into-limitations
3 How to quit your job, move to paradise, and get paid to change the world, https://problogger.com/how-to-quit-your-job-move-to-paradise-and-get-paid-to-change-the-world

Part Four
Build your free range escape hatch

18
Making a living without an office
(or a boss)

'Crazy ambition requires radical practicality. Otherwise, it's just... crazy.'

DANIELLE LA PORTE

So far you've been through a crash course in thinking like a free ranger: you've learned how to figure out what you want, busted the myths and discovered what you need (and what you don't). Now it's time to look at what it takes to launch out of there for real.

When I first decided to launch my own thing, I walked into a bookshop and bought a book about business building (yes, they had actual bookshops back then). I can't remember the book's name because I never finished reading it.

It was red, in a nice friendly workbook size, all about the steps you need to take in order to launch your venture in 20 weeks. Or something. All I remember is that I stopped reading it because it was overwhelming. And scary. Oh, and boring.

Man was that book boring.

First, I never thought I wanted a *business*. I wanted to make a living on my own terms, without an office or a boss – ever again. And yes, that meant being self-employed, but I hadn't gone into this because I loved the idea of being a (deep voice) 'business owner'. I wanted a nice life, you know? One where I could sleep in and not have to ask for permission to go on holiday, and where I got to do lots of things I loved. Somehow, that book (and the others on the shelves around it) forgot about us. Nothing in there was about the entire reason I wanted to make this change; what about the *life* that was meant to come after the job?

The book made it feel like launching a business was another world. One that I'd rather put to one side and get to later. *Someday.*

It wasn't until I got started that I realized something profound: conventional step-by-step books on starting a small business aren't about building a business. Most business-building products tell you how to create a business *shell.*

I would read things like: Step 1, Choose a name; Step 2, Register and fill in the paperwork; Step 3, Create a logo.

Fine. You can follow these steps, and you'll get something that looks like a nice professional business. Pity about the part where it's not bringing in money. The part where you learn how to do things in a smarter way than most struggling freelancers? Oh you can learn that later, the logic goes. No wonder people think that making money by yourself is a bit of a mystery.

So there I was, sitting with a pile of books that made me want to go to sleep (or panic), a bunch of things that I thought I *should* be doing, and a heap of 'argh' whenever I tried to work out which one to start with. And still no clue as to how any of it would bring in consistent good money.

What I know now

Back then, my vision of business was what I now call 'old-style business'. The difference between old- and new-style businesses is something you're going to find out about in the rest of this book.

If you're all up for the freedom of making a living by yourself, but feeling a bit *ugh* about this whole business-building malarkey, I guarantee you're thinking of old-style business. However, it is the new-style 'break the rules and make it yours' free range way of working that we're going to explore here.

But how will I pay the bills?

This question gives me the chills.

Imagine you're about to get on a plane with a trainee pilot. You already know the touchdown might be a tad bumpier than normal; sure, that's to be expected. However, the one question you don't want to hear him ask is *how can I make the plane stay in the air?*

That is the same as a free range fledgling asking about paying the bills. These are very good questions, yes, but both have an undertone of believing that is the very best you can expect. They suggest that paying the bills and somehow just staying afloat is all you can hope for.

If that's *all* you want, read a formulaic start-up guide, or go to a night class in a local college. There are a lot of ways to launch something average. But that's not what we're about.

Free ranging is about creating your ultimate life. Reaching your potential, building on that moment of magic you have to offer and creating a darn good income to boot. Freedom and fulfilment *and* a great income. No compromises.

Let's get real here

This stuff you're going to read about here works. But it doesn't work if you just go through the motions. Standing out, getting status, turning an idea into income – this is not a clever trick. I know it may sound fluffy, but the truth is you can't fake this. You cannot beige this up. Every time someone tries to pretend, and makes an inauthentic business decision to make a quick buck, that will be the decision that backfires.

You're going into this for a reason – for the life you want and to feel good about what you do, every day. I can give you the techniques to help this happen but there's a big part you have to play. This is about bringing the whole of you to the party.

At the end of the day, you're not building a business, you're creating a life. You in?

19
Why you don't need a business plan
(or an MBA)

'Nothing will ever be attempted if all possible objections must first be overcome.'

SAMUEL JOHNSON

The first step to working for yourself is often assumed to be 'Hole up alone in a room and write a long business plan'. Here's why you should be doing the exact opposite.

The 'research' myth

'Before I start properly I need to spend months researching, and write a detailed business plan.'

Myth buster

Get this: at your stage, most planning is really guessing.

Unless you're a fortune teller, long-term business planning is a fantasy. There are just too many factors that are out of your hands... Why

*don't we just call plans what they really are: guesses. Start referring
to your business plans as business guesses, your financial plans as
financial guesses, and your strategic plans as strategic guesses...*

*The timing of long-range plans is screwed up too. You have the most
information when you're doing something, not before you've done
it. Yet when do you write a plan? Usually before you've even begun.
That's the worst time to make a decision.*

> Jason Fried and David Heinemeier Hansson,
> founders of Basecamp and authors of ReWork.[1]

This applies double to free range businesses. You see, the main
purpose of a business plan is to help you raise funding by convincing someone else that your idea has potential. But as a Free Range
Human you're not looking for funding – you're starting small, so
the only thing that matters is real world results.

In other words: you don't need a long business plan. Yes, you
definitely should have a good idea where you're going. *But you can
do that on the back of a beer mat.*

In fact, spending months tinkering with a traditional business
plan might actively hold you back. I once heard an interview with
a guy called Andrew, whose first venture failed. When asked why
he said:

> *The biggest mistake we made was being completely encumbered by
> this vision of what I wanted it to be and taking 10 months to build
> the product, all the while making assumptions on what people want...
> You're way too dumb to figure out if your idea is good. It's up to the
> masses. So build that very small thing and get it out there.*[2]

That guy was Andrew Mason, founder of Groupon – one of the
biggest business successes of the decade. The above was the reason
why his first venture didn't work out... and why Groupon did.

What does this mean in practice? Well, if you want to educate
people, don't sit around figuring out how many folders you might
need next July. Instead, one evening after work, run a mini free
range project with 10 people. Find your first guinea pigs wherever

you can – maybe go to Meetup.com and start a new group, share in circles you are in, or ask your friends if they know anyone. Once you've done this you're not some person who will 'one day' start an education business. *You're actually in business.*

Mini case study

I'd been 'just thinking about' going free range for years and had been flitting from one idea to the other (always at the 'research' rather than the 'doing' stage). I'd typically say, 'I'm not ready yet', and overcomplicate things to the point of 'paralysis through analysis'. The free range approach has taught me how to simplify things, not to wait until everything is perfect, and take manageable steps in the right direction. When I actually put myself out there I gained a client out of the blue through Twitter, showing me that this is possible, and the steps I'm taking are being rewarded.

Mark Scanlon

Free range third way

Someone who takes this philosophy to heart is my friend Terri Belford. Some years back, Terri fell in love with a small seaside town. She wanted to get back into art, and this place seemed like the perfect location for a gallery. She found a venue in October... and made a commitment to open the gallery on Thanksgiving weekend at the end of November. Terri explains:

My only experience with the art business was selling my work at craft fairs when I was very young, so I spent the next few weeks going to open studios, chatting with artists and trying to figure out what sells. I gave myself a virtual MBA in the local art scene in a few weeks!

Because I don't believe in putting a lot of money into start-ups, I talked about 50 artists and craftspeople into working on a consignment basis – they lent me their art and they got paid when it sold. My son and I then headed to the lumberyard for plywood to build display pedestals. A few weeks later, we were in business.

Because Terri started free range style, she was able to adapt as she learned more on the ground. For example:

Some of the merchandise I started with turned out to be wrong for the clientele. But I didn't lose money. I simply returned it to the artists, grateful I hadn't invested upfront, and picked up more of the pieces that were selling well. Things took off from there.

Within the first couple of years, the business had outgrown its location, and I was earning a good income. When it was time to move on, I sold the business for a very nice six figures.

Terri didn't waste time worrying *I've never sold art professionally* or *I need to spend 12 months researching and creating a 100-page business plan*. She didn't do what other people might do: sink money into an expensive space, then try to raise funds to buy some art and then hope it sells. Actually, most people wouldn't do that: they would *think* they had to take that risky approach and then give up before starting.

Instead, Terri started small, learned fast, then flexed and adapted to what worked (and what didn't). You can do that too, even if it's in a side project while still in your job.

You see, it isn't about closing your eyes and jumping in blind. Free range successes evolve as an iterative process of learning and doing. *Learn an idea*, try it out, *learn a technique*, test again, *learn what works*, get out there... *oh look, you've launched and it's working!* That's a much smarter approach than spending months on a plan before you know what really works.

While it's up to you to do the 'doing', the rest of this book is going to help you with the 'learning'. I'm going to share strategies that will give you an edge in getting your free range journey off the ground and thriving. To get the most out of this, as you read, keep your mind ticking over to find ways of trying out these concepts by taking your own free range action, ASAP.

Tip

Beating the 'perfectionism freeze'

If you have a perfectionist streak (welcome to the club!) the concept of starting small and starting fast might be somewhat jarring.

Your Top Dog (the yappy inner critic you met earlier) would much prefer it if you holed up for 12 months writing a plan. He's likely to bark out messages about failure, and tell you that you *must* be certain that you will excel at every single step you take (even if that step is from the safety of your own computer). Top Dog's fear of failure is contagious. Here's how to deal with that.

When you start thinking, 'What if I waste time on this project and it doesn't work out?' or 'What if I start and I don't like it?', ask yourself another question: 'What is the cost of *not* starting?'

It is all too easy to forget that there's a cost to staying where you are now. That cost is your life, and specifically, your finite time.

When someone asks, 'What if something goes wrong?', my reply is: something's going wrong right now. Look at how long you have been dreaming about this. Consider how you feel. Consider that you are giving up the best cognitive hours of your life to something that doesn't feel right at all. *Consider that you already knew this all that time ago yet nothing has changed.*

Now ask yourself again: 'What has been the cost of *not* starting to date?' You may not know for sure whether it would have been a waste of time to start something but you do know the cost of not starting due to 'what ifs'. The only thing that will definitely not work out is doing nothing.

So don't get hung up on making a mistake. You're starting in a safe way – not putting your income on the line with each experiment! From now on, mistakes are just another way of learning what works and what doesn't. Remember, there's no prize for getting each step perfect first time around, and no penalty for having a mini project mess up.

It's fine to try something out before you're ready. In fact it's not just fine, it's essential. That's how every successful free ranger made their new life happen. Now it's your turn. As you read the rest of this book, get ready to take action and explore this new world on your terms.

20
Why you don't need to appeal to everyone

'When you innovate, you've got to be prepared for people telling you that you are nuts.'

LARRY ELLISON, FOUNDER, ORACLE

Here is where it all begins. Being clear on who you are (and who you're not) is the starting point of a successful free range career.

This is radically different to career-cage thinking. In the career-cage world, if someone doesn't love what you have to say, then that's a problem. The aim is to keep the peace, keep your head down and generally glide through the day and come out, you know, OK.

In the free range world, the opposite is true. So much so that years ago I opened up a fresh document and wrote the following words as a reminder for myself.

If you don't love what I have to say, here's what I want from you:

- I want you to hate me.
- I want you to say, 'That girl is not funny'.
- Say, 'Her fees are too high. What, she doesn't even offer regular, structured coaching? Who does she think she is?'
- I want you to say, 'Her language is unprofessional. She flaps her hands when she speaks. Can't *stand* her.'

- *Then, I want you to tell your friends how much you can't stand me.*

- When you run out of ammunition, tell them I have really bad hair.

Hate is similar to love. The person or brand you hate gets under your skin. They hit a sensitive spot that is beyond apathy. You feel something inside you start bubbling away. If someone hates me, no hard feelings; I'm just wrong for them – maybe just for now, maybe forever. Whatever. But the fact that someone can be incited to hate me means that my message is clear and strong enough that it will get under the skin of someone else – someone who will love my message, and feel I am speaking directly to them. If that's you, my message will hit a spot that is beyond apathy. You will feel something inside you start bubbling away... And that's a life-changing experience.

Scary stuff huh? But this might be the one thing that makes the difference between you shining... or failing.

Using the usual please-everyone approach, it takes just a few bad comments to topple your dreams. Aside from having an average, struggling business, when you pander to the beige-est common denominator, you end up unhappy: you end up trying to be someone you're not.

You know what? *Screw that.*

This is not about those people who don't get it. They were never going to become customers or loyal fans anyway. Pandering to them will just make you more average, more insipid and take you further away from the life you imagined. And the truth is, they won't love you, no matter what.

For every person who laughs at you when you are at your brightest, someone else loves you for exactly the same reason. The key to standing out and getting paid to be you is choosing those right people, and speaking to them and only them, in your full voice.

For example, Benny Lewis's language-learning approach has come under fire from the traditional language-learning community:

My approach is different to most linguists online. I am not interested in speaking the language perfectly, or becoming a literature expert. I want to get the learning over as fast as possible so I can go have fun on travels, and that's what my people want too, but it seems to offend the traditional experts.

They kind of hate me, yet that has helped me. All these bloggers who dislike what I do will write about me and link to me: 'Benny is an idiot because... link'! So they send traffic my way. They have helped expand my readership by not liking me!

The result is that Benny grew a popular language-learning business that earns him a full-time living.

In the next chapter you will see more on how choosing your people and appealing only to them gives you the edge to rise above the competition. For now, though, let's focus on you. This is not about following someone else's rules. This is about living life on your terms.

So, think of your free range idea (or ideas!) and the people you'd love to deliver them to, and consider this:

- What would you say to your people if you weren't worried about rejection?

- What possibilities would you create if you weren't worried about being 'odd'?

- Who would you be and what would you do if you were not afraid of other people's laughter?

Above all, tell me... *Who told you you'd be loved more if you were someone else?*

Big lives come from bold steps

I know you are reading this because you want something more in your life. The problem is, if you're holding back then there's no way of making this happen. Molly Mahar, coach and founder of Stratejoy, explains:

> *When we want to do something **more** or **bigger** but are held back by fear of putting ourselves out there, we are going to be trapped in a cycle of unfulfilled desire.*
>
> *When we care too much about what others might think of us, we're not going to make the changes or take the risks that are necessary to put our brilliance out in the world or simply be comfortable in our own skin.*

Result? We stay stuck.

And that sucks.

The part that sucks most is the thought that you might let other people's world view hold you back from doing your own thing.

The freedom you're looking for doesn't come with a simple business plan. It comes when you take a deep breath and choose who gets a say in your life... and who does not.

My journey from bland to bold

Reading back over this I can see you might get the impression that this is only a path for brave people with boundless self-confidence. It's not. *I know this because I've been the biggest people-pleasing approval junkie out there.*

Want to know how I, a chronic people pleaser, came to this place?

Unsurprisingly, I started out trying to appeal to 'as many people as possible'. I chose a wide niche (choosing them because I thought they were a 'smart business choice' not because I really wanted to work with them). I toned down my language to sound the way I thought I was supposed to. I deleted anything that might be off-putting to my harshest critics (who were mostly made up of the frowning committee of inner critics who tut-tutted in my head).

As a result, I ended up creating something that people thought looked 'very nice'.

Problem is, 'nice' doesn't pay the bills, and nice doesn't nurture your soul and your need to do something meaningful with your life. 'Nice' is code for *inoffensive* and *I am sure someone else will like it* (but then no one ever really does). Watch out if someone says your idea is *nice*. It means you're probably not going to sell much.

This wasn't the life and freedom I had envisaged when quitting my job.

I had a choice: look nice, stay in the middle, while holding myself back from being me, or take a deep breath, focus on a small group of people I care about, and dare to stand out.

One guess which one I chose.

You got it. I have no doubt that had I not started to say *no* to the parts that felt wrong and *yes* to the parts that felt right (but that some people might laugh at) then I wouldn't be writing this today. I'd have given up the dream, gone back to a job with a failed business, a cynical outlook and old hopes of freedom dashed.

It's not enough to have an idea and quit a job. *True liberation comes when you quit the shackles that you put on yourself.*

And that's how we stand up, stand out and bring things to life.

21
How to decide who gets to give you money

'The key to my success is I write to a specific audience (niche), and know how to find them.'
JOHN LOCKE (WHO SOLD OVER A MILLION FICTION EBOOKS WITHOUT A PUBLISHING DEAL)

If you're not going to appeal to everyone then who *do* you want to appeal to? That's an important question.

As we learned in the previous chapter, when you try to please everyone then you end up pleasing no one. Here's why this is. To please everyone, you have to leave out the good bits, the parts that spark and grab people. *Go generic and everyone will think your brand is nice, but no one will think it's for them.*

Imagine you're starting out as a massage therapist. Who do you want to appeal to? Say 'everyone' and the next question will be, 'how?' Your answer might be, 'I'll give good massages for reasonable prices.'

Congratulations. You are now competing with every massage therapist in the world.

Almost every person starting out in any industry says their point of difference is 'good service' and 'lower prices'. These days 'I'll treat you like an individual' is a popular add-on. If everyone offers these as their point of difference, then do you really think they're unique? No. Those three points have become *expected*.

If you want to stand out, you need something more.

Most people can only think of 'service' and 'price' as their differentiators because those factors are the only ones that appeal to *everyone*. If you aim for everyone you're right: you need to do more work for lower money as that's the only way in the crowded mass market.

Hmm, lower income for more work. How is that idea chiming with the life you want to create? Competing on price is a non-starter. For one thing you can be undercut all too easily. Someone offers your service a bit cheaper than you and you'll have to eat into your profits (read: lower your salary) to fight back.

The middle of the road is the most dangerous place to be (that's where you get run over by fast-moving traffic).

Going back to the massage business, what would happen if instead of targeting *everyone* you aimed at full-time parents who need a break? Or time-poor professionals who crave pampering in their lunch break?

When you choose a niche, you can start to differentiate what you do. For example, the parent niche could make their place child-friendly (or even child-free!). They can tailor packages to their market and speak about the situations that would lead to the parent needing a massage. They can talk about the guilt you might feel spending time and money on yourself yet how much better you can be for your child if you take that hour out for yourself. They could start a newsletter about self-care when you have kids. *They could end up writing a column about the topic in their local paper.*

Of course, not *everyone* would get this approach, so you'll miss out on the builder down the road who has a crick in his back from heavy lifting. But that will be more than made up for by the fact that your niche will flock to you.

That builder down the road has no reason to go to you if next door's massage service is cheaper: your mums do. If you don't specialize, you'll end up competing on price and then the only way is down.

Get this right and your people will go to you above anywhere else, then come back and tell their friends.

With a niche you rule the world. Specifically, *your niche's* world. You attract customers you love being around, you gain confidence (sorry Great Aunt Maude, you might think my business is a bit *out there* but you're not my niche), and you stand out. Result: more customers, more money and more satisfaction.

From burnout to brilliant: a real-life turnaround

Grace Marshall became a coach while juggling life with two young children. With sleepless nights and years of overwhelm behind her, and a coaching qualification and love for helping people under her belt, she decided to launch herself as a life coach specializing in burnout.

When I first met Grace she was working under the brand 'From burnout to brilliant', which she describes as 'for anyone who was feeling burned out. I didn't want to leave anyone out so I included everyone who might experience burnout, be it parents or teachers or doctors or preachers.'

Full marks for choosing a specific topic area – burnout – but without a niche of people, Grace's message was fragmented:

> *My website had a big list of burnout issues for everyone from students to professionals to grandparents. I kept thinking, 'They might be looking for X so I should put something on there about that!' No one bought my first offers because no one knew what I was about.*

Grace took some advice and looked at niching further:

> *I realized I really wanted to speak to parents who had been through what I had been through. So I niched down to parents and burnout. Then I niched further to mothers who were running their businesses.*

> *Every time someone signed up to my email list I asked, 'What's your biggest challenge in juggling business and family?' And the biggest*

was time: *the biggest topic was 'How do I find time with kids?' What if instead of everything 'burnout' related, I focused on productivity?*

Grace responded by launching her first productivity programme for 'mums in business' – and it filled faster than anything else she had offered.

It's funny, I resisted specializing in productivity for a while because I thought, I'm not a time management guru! But people kept asking me how do you do it, how do I fit it all in?

I got to thinking. I was running my business, a full-time parent to two young children, attending a leadership course, involved in the community, running a networking group in my local area and still having quality time with my husband and kids at the end of the day. Maybe I did know a bit about finding time!

So my productivity brand was that I'm not that organized super-mum type – far from it – but I need to get things done just like you, so here's how I've learned to deal with things. That appealed to people who are not naturally organized; they get that I know where they are coming from.

Remember the all-rounder myth (Chapter 7) where we think we have to be everything to everyone and resist the parts we do best? That's what was happening here. When people are asking you for help and you're saying, 'No I'm not good enough to talk about that', pay attention: your natural specialization and a great niche might be lurking beneath that.

Fear of niching

The three biggest resistances to niching are: 1) fear of missing out on work; 2) fear of being 'mean' by excluding people (particularly difficult for natural helpers!); 3) limiting yourself. Grace was held back by all three:

*It was difficult for me to niche; I didn't want anyone to feel left out,
I didn't want to miss anyone's business and I didn't want to miss out
on variety. The funny thing is that when people start working with
me I ended up covering all the issues in the sessions anyway, so I'm
getting more variety than I had before... and more work as well.*

By excluding people you end up reaching and helping more people
than ever.

Update

Years down the line, there is a twist to Grace's story. Doing the
above opened doors to a world she had never imagined.

Not long after I shared her story, Grace was offered a book
deal to write a popular book about productivity, and she started
speaking and meeting people in the field – including Graham
Allcott, the owner of Think Productive (a company that delivers
workshops and trainings to organizations on exactly this topic).
Graham loved her relatable style and they started working
together.

'Now I deliver workshops around the world,' Grace explains.
'I was in New York last month running a session for a big
company (quite a shift for someone with two kids in a small town
in England!), I collaborate on new courses and products, and I
love the way I get to work from home but with great people.

'The "mums in business" side isn't my focus so much now –
but starting out niching that way is exactly what got me here.
Without owning the productivity side and having a focused way
to talk about it I would never have got known or expanded into
this variety I have today – I would have been trying to 'be
everything' and in the process been nothing.'

This is not an unusual story: Grace's experience of getting
rolling with a topic (or people) that was close to her, opening the
door, and then evolving is the story of so many free rangers.

How to choose your niche

First notice the wording: you don't find your niche, you *choose* it. There is no one perfect niche out there waiting for you. Choose your niche based on what you want and what you love right now, then tweak it to fit, free range style.

Many people think a niche is like those demographic boxes you tick in a survey. So they might say 'my niche is women aged 25–45 (and maybe some men too)'. That's not a niche – that's the bulk of the purchasing population! What about their attitudes, their habits, the binding factors that mean they would probably get on if they met at a party? Attitude defines a niche as much as anything else.

Choose a niche for you

Quite possibly your first niche will be a group currently experiencing a problem you have faced, or the sort of people with whom you have spent a lot of time. It's easier to communicate with people whose situation you truly understand.

Once you have an idea of who you'd like to work with, describe them. What makes them different from the average person who would buy this product or service? What is their interest in your topic? Who are the people you don't want to work with? Be as descriptive as you want here. Remember: you're talking about real people, so get into the nitty gritty of how they think and feel. A rule of thumb is that you should never describe your niche with the words 'anyone who'. 'Anyone' is not a niche: get specific.

Make sure you are excited about working with these people (or on this topic). If you choose a niche purely on 'shoulds', such as 'I should work with corporates because they have the biggest budgets' *but* the thought of working with corporations makes your blood run cold, don't do it!

Much like the struggling person who came to me saying he wanted to target 'rich people' because they had a lot of money; it turned out he didn't know any 'rich people' and didn't feel comfortable hanging out with anyone who earned an above average salary. No wonder he wasn't getting very far. A 'hot market' is not hot if you don't know anything about it.

This doesn't mean being stupid, of course. If your niche is broke and can't or won't pay, then avoid it unless you want to end up the same way. But don't assume you have to hit the top end of the market to make a great living. If you love your niche, can speak their language and they can pay... you're off to a great start.

Once you know who you want to work with, the next question is: how are you going to present yourself to them?

22
How to brand like a rock star

'Find out who you are and do it on purpose.'

DOLLY PARTON

I was going to open this chapter with examples of fabulous rock star brands and what we can learn from them, such as how Lady Gaga grabbed the most successful female recording artist mantle by shunning the usual boxes, doing her own thing and creating just for her ultra-loyal tribe.

But there are hundreds of articles on that already. To me, there is a more interesting part to branding, a quieter part that most people don't talk about. And that is this simple truth: *branding like a rock star takes guts.*

You don't need 30 million Instagram fans, your tribe's name tattooed on your arm, or an over-the-top music brand to brand like a rock star. But you do need the guts to not blindly follow the herd. And that's the opposite of what you've been taught to do in career-cage land.

Surrounded by pressure to be self-effacing and fit in, when it comes to explaining who you are and what you're about in your business, the temptation is to squish down the message that's bubbling up and replace it with a message that feels more acceptable. Fitting in and toning it down may sound like an easy route to success but nothing could be further from the truth. Follow the herd, and your powerful roar can dwindle down to a mini mewl.

Branding like a rock star means more than a logo or a gimmick. It means coming out of hiding, stepping up and being you in shining lights.

Tip

In the same way that great music isn't all thumping rock, great branding doesn't have to mean 'brash and loud'. Not if being that way isn't real for you.

Just as fake is telling a thoughtful quiet introvert that 'authentic branding' means making videos of you standing on the edge of a cliff, being as 'in your face' as possible. Yes, that's a great, brave, gutsy approach for someone who knows that represents a big part of them. But if it's not you? Then that's not brave. That's putting a layer over who you are, being who you think you have to be in order to be good enough to do this.

More to the point, doing that because that's what all the cool kids are doing is not 'branding like a rock star' – it's more 'branding like a tribute band'... One that struggles to get gigs anywhere without sawdust on the floor – and doesn't know why, because don't they look *just like the other guys who are selling out stadiums?* The mistake they made was thinking branding was fake, or that it was a copy-and-paste job.

But branding that hits home is far from that. It uncovers what's really there so that others can see it (*before* spending loads of time with you).

Quiet, quality, and real can be as powerful as fast and loud. What counts is what lets your people get you and know you are for them. In short: don't buy into the idea that there's only one way to be. Branding has more than one note. It's up to you where you sit in that.

The power of branding as you

A great example of this is Luke Milton. With a background as a professional rugby player in Australia, when Luke started thinking about starting his own personal training business it would have been easy for him to brand like, well, every other trainer out there at the time. In other words, 'Taking this fitness thing so seriously you forgot to laugh'. Problem was, that wasn't Luke at all:

> *The whole reason I loved playing rugby was the camaraderie – like having a family to go to who you had a great time with.*
>
> *More to the point I'm Aussie; we like to joke and laugh and not take ourselves too seriously – we make everyone welcome. What if we could combine that feeling with a top training session – where you had a great time, made new mates and also got fit?'*

So one day he gathered together people in Central Park in NYC for a bootcamp – and called it 'Training Mate'. That evolved to a business in Sydney and Los Angeles, with classes with names like 'Thunder Down Under', a kangaroo painted on the wall, and the most fun, life-affirming sessions you'll ever go to.

I remember my first session there: I had just landed in LA from London (aka not the fittest by LA standards!) – and right at the point I'd usually give up, Luke cracked a joke about 'Plank Sinatra'. I was hooked.

These guys weren't putting on some fake façade to fit into their serious field in an image-conscious city – they were just clear on who they were and very, very good at what they do. Walk into Training Mate and you're treated like an old friend – from the class names to the experience (where you hear more bad jokes from the instructor than you would at a stand-up gig) their brand is clear.

As a result, Luke has gone from someone who could have been yet another ex-footballer doing personal training, to creating a thriving community and business that keeps growing. It's an approach to fitness that has impacted thousands of regular people, led to one of the most booked workouts in town[3] – and recently it even landed him on television as a top celebrity trainer.

Looking at this from the other side it's easy to think, 'Well that's a great brand, it's *obvious* he should have gone for it!' But think of all the *reasons why not* that could have been there at the start – the thoughts of 'But shouldn't I be like the others?' or 'Does this look serious enough?' It's easy to undervalue what we have – and to focus on who might not get it. But they've had more reach, and impacted more people, by showing up as *them* than they would have by trying to play it safe.

Your brand is more than a name

To me, the most important part of Luke's story is not the name. That's one part of the picture, but it's the rest that brought it to life.

You see, a brand is every single experience that people have of you. From, yes, your brand name, but also what you say, how you say it, what you offer, how you offer it, who your 'people' are. The feel of the experience – are you about inspiration, education, seriousness, lightness, setting off a flare and shining brightly or toning it down and existing gently? How do people experience you, and how do you respond to them?

A good example of this is Ms Cupcake's brand. The focus is passion, fun and old-fashioned *generosity*. Generosity comes across in the bold, colourful website, the warm welcome at their stall and shop, and most importantly, in the cakes themselves. The first thing you notice about her cupcakes are their generous size: oversized creations with miles of beautiful frosting.

'I know most people can't eat one of my cupcakes by themselves,' Melissa explains. 'Most people share one, and that's part of the experience of Ms Cupcake. The brand is big, fun and generous.'

Many people see branding as false or misleading, but good free range branding is the exact opposite. A great brand takes what you have to offer and puts it on the outside so people 'get' you and your offering, even before they buy from you.

A brand name is just one part of it. Having said all that, your brand name is the first impression people have of you. It is also the ongoing image people hold of you, and will impact on what you do. Here's how to choose yours.

Exercise: Seven steps to choosing your first brand name

1   Write out a list of 20–30 words that describe what you're really about. I put this challenge to a client running a relaxation and alternative medicine practice and he came up with words such as 'authenticity', 'calm', 'change', 'renewal' and 'fresh'. Some of those words are obvious to his field, and others are a little more personal to him.

2   Review your list. Now, cross out any words you put there because you thought you 'should' (hint: those are the words everyone will be using), not because they are really, really core to you.

3   Shortlist. Write your favourite three to five words at the top of a page with a column underneath each one.

4   Brainstorm. Under each word, brainstorm brand names. Don't edit, just write ideas as they come. You're looking for something that captures both the feel of your approach and personality as well as being immediately understandable to someone who hears it.

5   Sanity check. Is this 'too smart' or 'wonderfully sticky'? A great brand name should connect with your audience the moment they hear it (ie be 'sticky'): you should not need an 'About' page to explain it before people get it. It's fine to have a hidden meaning as a secondary benefit but if your people don't connect with the name immediately, they won't stick around to 'get' the rest of it.

6 Personality check. Is this really *you*? Are you happy going out and being this person? Remember: there's no such thing as a good brand name. There is only a brand name that is good for *you*. Choosing a name purely because it sounds clever is like choosing a shirt because it is trendy and looks good on the model – but when you put it on it makes you look terrible. Your brand should not make you feel you have to be someone you're not. (If you have to constantly check with your brand to have permission before you speak, that's a hint that your brand is wrong.) If you're not happy being that brand, you'll hold yourself back.

7 Be prepared to change your brand name. You may have noticed that I said your *first* brand name. That wasn't a mistake. Your first brand name probably won't be your last. Most people play with a safe option before finding their true voice. The biggest insights will come on the ground.

Remember, you don't have to spend a million dollars rebranding. I rebranded my business for the price of a few lattes.

As you get into motion, your true brand – name and all – will emerge in a way you can never achieve thinking from the sidelines. For example, Free Range Humans was not my first brand name – but I'm glad I didn't wait for the perfect brand name before I launched, as I would never have found that name if I hadn't been out there, doing this for real.

Tip

Why you don't need a fancy logo

You can start a great brand without a bespoke logo. I've seen people waste months choosing a logo, yet when was the last time you bought something just because it had a clever logo? A logo is the last thing you should be worrying about in your first few months; write out your name in a decent font and get going. You can always come back to it when you're actually up, running and profitable.

If in doubt, take inspiration from Deloitte. Their logo is just their name written in a regular font with a dot at the end – and that hasn't stopped them being one of the biggest consultancies in the world.

23
How to stand out from the crowd

'If you don't get noticed, you don't have anything. You just have to be noticed, but the art is in getting noticed naturally, without screaming or without tricks.'

LEO BURNETT

A little story for you:

When Cathy was 14, she was desperate to be an individual. She didn't want to be just one of the herd, so Cathy made an effort to dress differently. She wore her hair shorter, her clothes looser, her jewellery bolder. Problem was, outside of her social group, no one noticed. To adults, she was indistinguishable from the rest of the 14-year-old crowd. Sales assistants treated her just like everyone else. Cathy got more and more frustrated – and no one wants to see a frustrated teenager!

One day, in art class, her teacher asked everyone to write out a paragraph describing their own personal style. Cathy wrote: 'I don't follow trends. I wear my jeans looser than Sara's, my hair shorter than Ramona's and my jewellery bolder than Bella's.'

Cathy's teacher read this, and wrote the following comment: 'If you truly don't follow trends, then why did you use what others wear to define your style?'

That was when it hit Cathy. She has *been following trends: she was following them to define who she was not. Her jeans were not like Sara's; her hair was not like Ramona's; her jewellery was not like Bella's. But she had no idea how to describe herself without reference to other people.*

Cathy would never stand out as a real individual when her only approach was 'to do something a bit different from the crowd'.

This is the story of a 14-year-old girl. It's also the story of almost every new business that says *I want to stand out from the crowd.*

There are three factors involved in standing out from the crowd

Figure 23.1   Stand out from the crowd: three factors to consider

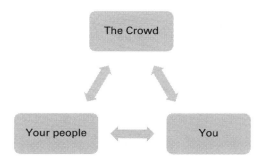

The crowd means your competition. *You* means you personally, your brand, what you offer, what you say, and how you communicate. *Your people* means your niche, or more simply, the people who you want to buy some of that great stuff you have to offer.

When you think about standing out from the crowd, where do you start? With the crowd, with you, or with your people?

1 Most people start with the crowd.

2 Most people start by looking at their competitors as their very first step.

3 Most people struggle to stand out for this very reason.

When your website is a copy (with minor variations) of someone else's, when your language is 'industry gobbledygook' (like every other struggling business), and when other people's products, services, attitudes and prices define what you think you are 'allowed to do', then you are behaving like Cathy. You are always defined by someone else (often, ironically, by someone else who is struggling). Start from the crowd, and your business runs a high chance of being a pale copy of everyone else's.

How to stand out (by being more you)

Don't start with 'the crowd'. They come later, once you have something to say and someone to be. For now, start with two factors: you, and your people. Your aim is to be the most attractive to that sliver of society who you really want to work with.

You don't need a radical new idea for this. You simply need to embrace your 1%.

The 1%/100% model of standing out

How different do you think you need to be in order to stand out? Do you think you need to be completely new and fresh? Have a new niche no one else is touching? Pioneer a new field?

That sounds like a lot of hard work. What if, instead, you only had to find your 1% difference?

The 1%/100% model is an approach I designed to articulate the large impact of small differences.

I was discussing this idea with a friend over coffee and our choice of meeting place illustrated this perfectly. When I'm in the UK and buying coffee from a chain, I always choose Caffè Nero. Why? Well, it's not just that they do good coffee:

- It's that they use actual real chocolate in their hot chocolates rather than synthetic 'chocolate flavouring'.

- It's the fact that they always have two jugs of water on the counter, next to a stack of fresh glasses, there for you to help yourself.

● Real chocolate. Free water. That's what I call a 1% difference.

However, that 1% difference gets 100% of my business. When you're a small business, 100% of someone's business is excellent. Start thinking of your people now. What are they really buying when they buy what you are thinking of offering? (Hint: it's not just the coffee.)

What 1% difference will equal 100% of their individual custom to you? 1) It might be the language you use – you're far more friendly/professional/informal/intellectual/down to earth (delete as appropriate) and that resonates with your people; 2) it might be that your brand feels more 'kick ass women' rather than 'soft, pink and girly'. Or vice versa.

Whatever it is, there are two rules on making the 1% difference work for you.

Rule 1: you need to be 1% different on something that the people you are comparing yourself against don't treat as important

Seth Godin puts it well:

> *You don't get someone to switch because you're cheaper than Walmart. You don't get someone to switch because you serve bigger portions than the big-portion steakhouse down the street... Instead, you gain converts by winning at something the existing provider didn't think was so important.*[4]

I bet that other coffee chains don't think a constant supply of water and a certain type of chocolate is that important. And they are right too – it's not crucial for them or their people. It won't stop someone dominating the café market and having their own loyal fans.

But these details are a 1% difference that will convert 100% of that type of person who does find it important, and that's enough of a market for a whole other business.

Rule 2: your 1% difference should come from YOU

Defining your identity and brand by comparison to that of your competitors is not what I'm talking about when I say find your 1% difference. The 1%/100% model is about identifying the points where you are *naturally different* and breathing life into them so they become bigger and clearer.

So, are you an image consultant who is approachable and warm or super-efficient and bluntly honest? Are you an image consultant who kicks butt on corporate wardrobes or changes the lives of those whose cupboards are packed with clothes they wore 10 years ago (but who have nothing to wear today)? Do you make me feel sexy or relaxed?

There is no right answer – only the truth about who you are versus the person you think you should be.

Remember:

- Standing out is not a gimmicky add-on.

- Being outstanding is not an afterthought tacked on by a marketing department.

- Putting your best self out there is the most generous thing you can do. *Hiding is not a contribution.*

You don't have to be a certain type of person to succeed in your industry. Is your product that much more advanced or is it simpler? Are you the one who hugs people better or the one who goes 'bang' with the raw truth? Whatever the answer, don't hide it. That's your secret superpower.

Who am I again? (the problem with personal branding)

There are a dozen versions of you that bubble up in any one day. One moment you feel serious and analytical and another you feel playful and irreverent. Which of these personas is the 'real you'?

The answer: all of them.

A more useful question is, which *version* of you do you want to be in your business? 'Authentic' does not mean 'show up and act the way you feel on the day, one moment being sunny and the other shouting at everyone'. Unless your personal brand is to be wildly unpredictable, this is not a great move.

A great personal brand means taking a certain aspect of your personality and putting it on speed. Whether it's something simple like being the 'approachable, friendly' one in a field that can be a bit pretentious (I have a friend who made a whole career out of being that person!) or whatever is true for you, owning it rather than hiding it is one of the smartest free range moves you can make.

Mini case study

It took me a while to 'get' the point that apparently my smile is a big part of my 1% (in my career coaching business). One coachee said at the start of a session, 'I want THAT smile you have today!' When I talked to people about what drew them to me, it's one of the first things they mentioned; even my test clients said, 'Oh, it's your smile and your energy'. But I didn't consider taking this seriously and including it in my brand… I had a serious corporate career for years, how could my smile count? But it does.

It's obvious to others, but for yourself you sometimes have to go into detective mode.

Nicole Est

Standing out often means taking what you might sometimes see as weaknesses (or 'not enough') and instead of stuffing them away and pretending to be someone else, turning them into advantages. This is not something you layer on top of who you are – but rather something that's already there and that you 'own' in order to let people see it more clearly. That is when you truly stand out, free range style.

Why does knowing your 1% make a difference? Well, not only does it give you clues as to what to do *more* of, it also means you don't accidentally minimize your best moments because you never realized they counted.

So stay curious to this as you go! (If you aren't sure where to start, a simple shortcut is to do a good personality assessment as outlined in Chapter 7. That outside view can start to give you a steer on your 1% differences.)

Mini case study

I was trying to blend in and be more 'polished' to be taken seriously in my new industry (interior design). This book helped me to make a virtue of my idiosyncrasies instead.

I started sharing images of my most colourful designs, which were different from most of the other companies in my area. I'm also not that technical so I hand-draft my design plans, but rather than apologize for not using CAD (the industry standard computer program), I weaved this into my brand image – artisanal, hand-crafted. I even changed my business name to reflect this!

Now I'm attracting clients who want me for my style, and steadily growing my reputation and audience. I've been shortlisted for an award, got press, and won a place to design a room set at a big design show. I even got the confidence to start running workshops teaching my design process to homeowners!

No more trying to fit in with the usual 'beige' bling – when I started being myself, the client enquiries came in. I've never been a typical 'business type', but now I've found a way to make things work as me.

Zoe Hewett

24

The three Free Range Styles

(or: how to get clients without paying for advertising... and without having to become someone you're not)

Over the last few chapters we've talked about standing out and doing things as you in terms of who you work with and how you come across to them.

But what about when it comes to how to run your business? How do you get clients and bring in an income – without spending a ton on advertising or having to pretend to be someone you're not (especially if you're not a classic 'business type')?

That's what this chapter is all about. As you'll find here, the answers to what to focus on to get clients flowing to you have less to do with the sort of business you have, less to do with whatever is trendy, and a whole lot to do with *who you are*.

Because the funny thing is, we do all this work to craft something to you – from choosing *what* you do (your idea), to *who* you do it for (your people), to *how you come across*. But so often, when it comes to how you bring in clients and money, *boom*, all that personalization gets left behind. It suddenly feels like you'll have to put on a mantle of someone else's personality (maybe someone more 'out there' and social – or maybe someone more structured and technical) to have half a chance of making it.

And there are plenty of messages out there ready to back that up – I bet you've seen ads saying things like '*Follow the exact 5 steps I took to get thriving income!*' (Aka: 'Be a cookie-cutter version of me and everything will work out!')

Those messages are tempting, right? I loved that one-size-fits-all idea at first... but soon noticed a problem. No matter what strategy was being taught (or who was teaching it, or how many millions they'd made), time after time I'd see the same thing: three people, all equally smart and dedicated, would start down the same path with the same tools – but two would hit a wall while one would thrive. *Why?*

That's what this chapter is here to answer with you – so you can fall into the latter camp!

I first noticed this when, not long after quitting my job, I joined a mentorship group. From day one, I thrived. Everything the person at the front of the room said clicked, I'd take action on it, and things would shoot ahead. I made back my investment in *weeks* (and it's still delivering to this day).

But next to me were two lovely, smart, dedicated people – who had joined the group over a year before me, and couldn't get *anything* working for them. How could it be that they'd try and stall, while I'd just find it *easy*?

Today, I know that this was no accident. Today, I know that the leader of the group was teaching what worked for her – *and she and I happened to share the same 'Free Range Style'*. What we were taught in that room was bang on for *that* style – but not for the styles of the other two people.

Of course, none of us knew this. But I wish we had – because fast-forward years later and both those people are thriving doing what they love, with clients and income flowing...

But it took them an extra 5+ years of work and significant investment on the wrong paths to happen on the right one for them.

They were not less capable than I was – they were just in the wrong room for them. I'd like to save you that trouble and get you into the right 'room', without 5+ years of waiting.

Working this out alone can be a lot of guesswork, so this chapter gives you an easier way by introducing you to the *Free Range*

Styles. These Styles start to answer the question: when it comes to attracting clients and income, why do some approaches work for some people but not others (and most of all, which will work best for you)?

You can't always tell how people *really* bring in clients and income just by looking at their website (in fact it's often a red herring!). So think of this chapter as your friendly free range detective, taking you in the side door and showing you the themes of how things work for real people (who are thriving in what they do)... and it starts with identifying your Free Range Style.

What are the Free Range Styles?

The three Free Range 'styles' are:

Figure 24.1   Free Range Styles

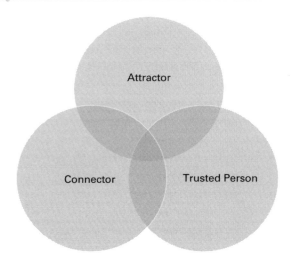

I'll explain what each of these mean in a moment. But first, to be clear, each Style focuses on one thing: *where clients and income come from*.

Your Style doesn't tell you what sort of business you should do, what products/services you can offer or how successful you can be! This doesn't put you in a box – instead it helps you filter *out* the noise that isn't so much 'you', to let you home in on activities that will work more naturally for you when it comes to attracting clients and consistent income.

Here's a quick overview of each Style:

Attractor: An Attractor is the magnet. They are the one whose brand or name people gravitate to, *even without them having met or been connected to those people.* The Attractor is the name who is out front. They (or their creation) need to be visible. Attractors attract people not just to themselves but to story, products or ideas. Attractors who have never done their own thing and don't yet have a 'magnet' can be spotted as they are often fascinated with using story, presentation, and communicating ideas in a way that makes an impact – and they do so naturally. (Their career highlights often happen when they get to use story, or present ideas, in that way.)

Connector: Sometimes mistaken for an Attractor, a Connector is best when chatting. If the feel of an Attractor is a magnet, the feel of a Connector is movement – they tap into their relationships as well as going out and creating new ones and that's where their income comes from. Often more extroverted than the other Styles, they are often initiating contact – they want to know people, so they send that email, set up that coffee (but they do so in a natural way, so it doesn't feel 'sleazy', and as soon as people meet them, they just want to know them more). They are the person who can walk into a room and come away with five new friends (*and barely even notice they did that*). Their primary free range income tends to come 1) by working directly under or with other people's established brands and followings, or 2) by using their ability to connect with those who have access to the right groups of people, to meet people who are then drawn to what they are offering under their *own* brand or name.

Trusted Person: A Trusted Person is one of the most common yet
least known attraction profiles. A Trusted Person does *not* need
what we conventionally think of as a brand (or a following) in
order to make things work (and in fact can be held back by the
attempt to create one). While the feel of a Connector is bright
motion, the feel of the Trusted Person is rootedness. Often more
introverted, their income comes when people trust a) their
expertise and b) the personal relationship. Most often found in
deep one-on-one conversations, these are the people who do
best with qualifications, expertise and quiet interactions.

Exercise: Which of these Styles feels *most* like you?

This is not about which you think is more worthy or which you
should be (every field has people of all three Styles thriving in it!)
– it's about which, from the work you have been doing on
uncovering who you are, feels like the *most* natural fit.

Write your answer here:

_____

_____

Wait, I think I'm two – or even all three!

You're right. We all have a piece of each of them – however, one
will be dominant and the other two less so.

Which is why I say your *main* attraction Style. Knowing your
main Style doesn't stop you dipping into the others here and there,
but it does help you think more clearly about where to put the
majority of your 'growing this thing' time in a way that works for
you.

So write down which feels most like you for now, and read on.

> **Tip**
>
> As you read through, don't dismiss an idea for being too 'obvious'. That feeling is often a hint that it is in line with your best strengths and flow.

The best way to understand the Styles is to see them in action. So let's look at real-life examples of three people thriving in the same industry... but with three different Styles. The examples are all from the same 'topic area' as it's easier to see differences between the Styles that way; however, be assured this works across all topics and types of free range career.

You can either read through each Style or feel free to flip ahead to your dominant Style without getting in too deep on the others. If you want more, at the end of the chapter is a bonus resource that dives deeper into each one (and shares more examples from different areas).

Attractor (aka The Magnet)

Figure 24.2 Attractor

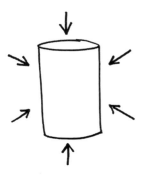

This one's my Style! As we've now (virtually) met, let's keep it simple and use me as an example here.

As an Attractor, I make my income primarily through people hearing about and being attracted to my products and offering – via my brand and my visibility in speaking, in interviews and on-line. The more visible my work and I are, the more easily everything flows. But at the start I wasn't even slightly keen to admit that.

When I started out, I was a master at hiding. I had a sense that being 'seen' or having a brand presence was almost like cheating, or would require me to be fake. My first website had only a tiny photo of me (which looked nothing like me), no way to get a 'taste' of what I did or how I thought, and little visibility…

And, unsurprisingly, almost no clients and customers.

However, that turned around when I started to do the things that matter to Attractors – such as growing a base of people who love what you have to say or offer.

For me, I did this through writing (with actual personality in it) and audio/videos, and starting to have content and a perspective that stuck with people. People would see a talk/video series/audio of mine online, it would click with them, they would sign up to my email lists, get to know me through that and often end up becoming a client (or send it on to their friends who would also come on over) – that's how things grew without paying for advertising!

Then when you want to offer something, you don't have to put up flyers, or rush desperately between networking meetings – you always have new people listening, keen and ready for more.

Dos and don'ts

As an Attractor you get clients and income based on how strongly people are magnetized to you (or your brand, or your offers).

What you need:

- To have your 'inside' clear on the outside so people can be drawn to you as the magnet.

- To know how you come across purposefully.

- An understanding of how the 'outside' of something looks, how it will come across to people who it is right for, and the communication to back that up (key for Attractors).

- A clear path from interest to purchase. As an attractor you are the magnet; no one else is bringing your income to you, so this is essential. See the bonus below for a walk-through of one way to do this.

What you can't hide behind:

- Certifications or length of experience.

- Knowing a few people.

- Being the 'best-kept secret' in your field (unless you use that overtly in your branding of course!).

Bonus

For a walk-through of one Attractor-friendly way to grow consistent income (without paying for advertising), download a bonus chapter here: http://frh.me/bonusconsistentincomechapter

---

Now, there are variations within this Style – for example, not all Attractors need a website to pull this off, and not all need to be as 'personally' visible as this (for them it's their *products or ideas* that are visible). Your Style gives you the compass, but you can always refine the *exact* path from there, this time knowing you're headed in the right direction.

For more on starting and growing as an Attractor, see the resource at the end of this chapter where I go into more detail about each style, including finding your flow and getting started.

Connector

Figure 24.3   Connector

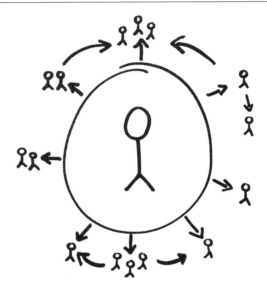

Selina Barker – the coach you've met at several points in this book – has, with seeming ease, become one of the most respected names in her space. She's been quoted in at least six books, co-founded courses and events that reached thousands, been booked up with clients for a long time, co-founded a second business (Project Love) with a physical product that has been stocked in shops across the country...

Oh and she built up this full-time thriving free range life without a 'brand', and was full-time for years *without* relying on her website (or a traditional following) to make the majority of her income.

How did she do this? By being a *Connector*.

'My superpower is chatting,' Selina explains. 'I've built my whole free range career through chatting and making friends.'

When I asked Selina the killer question – 'Where has the majority of your free range income come from?' – her answer was 'Relationships and partnerships – my first clients came from talking to people around me about what I was doing, and I have spent my career partnering with people who have a following.'

This allowed Selina to grow a full-time income without having a 'brand' that people knew (until many years in!).

However, when she decided to start a second business and *did* want the brand to be known she did that the Connector way too:

In my second business (Project Love) my partner Vicki and I are both Connectors and, while we do have a brand, our business success still comes from getting out there and making friends. The relationships we grow through chatting and genuinely being interested in people lead to partnering with brands, to hundreds of people doing our courses, to major press – and most of our income.

A thriving Connector is most likely found interacting with people, be it in conversation, in communities, at events, hosting dinners or building relationships (online or offline) – this is where their opportunities (and clients) most naturally come from.

As Selina says, 'When I chat with people, things work; when I start worrying about being a 'magnet' and sit around trying to tweak things, things stop.'

However, in the past Selina spent a long time not realizing that her Style was valid:

Even though I was my own boss, I had this sense that I'd just been playing and one day I'd do things 'properly' – meaning more like the people I was seeing out there.

I thought that 'real business' was about having a huge following and a proper sales funnel and a perfect website – all of that – but in reality, that's never where my full-time income has come from! It is, however, where most of my stress-filled time and investment has gone over the years.

That's why the Free Range Styles were so powerful for me, because I finally saw that what I was doing was a real approach – and that what I'd always done naturally, was what I should do more of!

Wait, but how can the Connector Style work for consistent income? Turns out, pretty well. As Selina says:

> *For many years I was full-time with hardly any following and my income was still consistent because of people I got to know. I could tap into their following, or do something jointly, or simply have them turn into clients.*
>
> *I didn't have most of those contacts when I started – but my best time investments have been growing these relationships. That is what has created security for me. I only wish I'd been told at the start that was a valid way to do things.*

Dos and don'ts

What you need:

- To be in conversations.
- To get into motion with a project or two that's in line with where you want to be. This gives you something to talk about and a way to connect with people.
- To work with others. Doing things all alone doesn't work for a Connector (it's hard for many people, but is kryptonite for a Connector).

What you can't hide behind:

- Having a nice website or paying someone a lot of money for branding.
- Status indicators like a book or a qualification (those can help with your connections, yes, but they aren't the primary thing that will bring in a Connector's income).
- A laptop screen. If a connector is alone, they aren't growing, so above all don't hide away.

Now we come to the final Style. If the Connector is the most extroverted, you're about to meet the more introverted.

Trusted Person

Figure 24.4 Trusted Person

When Jeanne started her own thing in her mid-twenties, she was in her element. She created a profitable and successful service business in her home town, loved every part of it for years – and at the end sold it for a sum of money she never would have dreamed of. From here she moved to the corporate environment, but after a while saw that wasn't a good fit for her. So Jeanne decided it was time to be free range again.

She read up about starting your own thing today, and thought, 'Well an online business (with virtual products) looks like a smart idea right now, I'll do that.'

In her diligent way, Jeanne learned every piece of the picture: she ended up with a neat website, a funnel, a brand, systems (and a big corkboard on the wall mapping out the entire process)... oh, and absolutely no clients or customers.

Jeanne was trying to be like so many of the 'visible' people she was seeing out there – and as a result had been putting her time and energy into trying to do things like an Attractor, when really she was a Trusted Person.

So what did she do differently with *that* information?

Instead of focusing on tinkering with a brand (that no one was looking at) and a mailing list (that I barely had anyone on) I went to where people who needed my solution already were. I found a platform where (many!) people were actively looking for coaches to work with and I could respond to them individually.

I laser focused on individual conversations, listening intently to what their problem was, and focused on solving it for them. I also focused on getting testimonials for my expertise, even if it meant doing something for free – and at first it did. That's when things started to shift.

Finally I was able to actually spend my time doing the work I wanted to do with clients – the work I loved doing! – rather than going around in circles trying to attract them in the first place, which never felt right for me.

From there Jeanne got referrals ('my income is consistent and growing, as each client seems to lead to another!') and she had to keep raising her prices to keep up with demand.

Now while this might sound like a slower way to start, it was the opposite for Jeanne. Remember: she went from stuck for over a year, to full-time (more than replicating her corporate income) within months by focusing on what worked for her 'Trusted Person' Style.

Dos and don'ts

What you need to thrive:

- Expertise in an area (your topic, your craft, your service).
- Referrals and testimonials (proof of others' trust in you).
- One-on-one conversations (that build trust in you and your ability).
- An understanding of your client/customer needs and how to expertly provide them.

What you can't hide behind:

- A brand or neatly constructed website (that has no one coming to it!).

- Describing the outside without showcasing your inside (find ways to show high value in practice).

When stuck:

- Think of *one* person you can reach at a time rather than endlessly trying to craft a message to reach 10,000 people. (Note: this does not mean you stay small. One of those people might be an Attractor with access to those 10,000 people, while another might be a client who ends up referring you to many others.) When in doubt, think individual connection first.

Turbo boost for Trusted People
(trust with one that can lead to many)

Want to reach even more people without having to become someone else?

Here is the twist to this story: Jeanne Patti is not just *a* Trusted Person… she is *my* Trusted Person on this topic.

Jeanne has worked closely with me on the Styles from the start: using her deep expertise in temperament, personality and systems she vetted them, tested them on her clients to be sure they worked for a wide range of people (and also combined her talent at making complex ideas simple alongside my Attractor Style of making an idea 'land' and stick with more people).

Because of this you know her *without* her having to spend ages building up a huge following first (a fact that Jeanne assures me she is delighted by).

Bottom line: think deep rather than wide. Trusted People aren't about 'spreading the net'. Their income comes and grows from depth of individual relationships.

Bringing this to life

Remember, these Styles (which I also call Attraction Models) don't define the work you do, or how you deliver it – they're just *about your most natural way of bringing in clients and income.* These are all very real paths thousands of people use to get consistent income and grow from there.

No Style is better or worse than the others. There are people with equal amounts of success, happiness, freedom and whatever else you are seeking using each Style – *but* each only works smoothly for that type of person.

Going back to the start, look at Selina (Connector) and I (Attractor) and things look similar from the outside – but the inside is quite different. When she tries to do things like me, everything slows. If I try to be like her, sure I can have a good time and get plenty of inspiration (my best ideas come from chatting!) – but going into Attractor mode is where my *impact and income* shoot ahead.

In short – while of course you can use the other Styles to enhance what you do (you aren't just one thing after all!), when it comes to bringing in income and clients, your primary Style is where to put the *majority* of your focus.

While most people find this out after a long time of trial and error, as of right now you have a very human framework to help you better filter where to put your time and headspace – without getting lost in the 1001 conflicting should-dos out there.

So from today, *don't* listen to Top Dog saying you have to sink most of your time into an approach that you can now see is not in line with your Style. *Do* look out for where you might use your Style even 10 per cent more. Those two steps, done consistently, will have you ahead of the pack.

Styles bonus

Want more on this (from working out your Style, to using it in your own way, and what it means in practice for you)? Click over to the special bonus resources on the Free Range Styles where my favourite Trusted Person Jeanne and I talk you through this topic in more depth! http://frh.me/stylesbonus

The Ladder Game

While the free range approach is to start from who you are, it is also realistic. Yes, start from who and where you are and craft the best solution you can… but don't let the search for perfection stop you from taking action!

If you can't see a way forward purely in your Style, go forward by playing what I call the 'Ladder Game'.

Here you get a full 10 points for moving 100 per cent in your Style, *but you get 0 points for no action*.

So if you imagine that an action is a 6 or 7 out of 10, but your other option is 'do nothing' then go for the 7. Now you're further up the ladder than those who waited for perfection to show up on a white horse – which means you're more likely to get there in the first place.

(You're also far ahead of those who haven't read this book and think they have to pick something off the shelf and fit themselves into it – they're often sitting with a 2 or 3.)

In short: do your best to find the *most* 'you' way and get the input to bring it to life. (For a start, make use of the resources above!) But *don't* freeze on the way… and don't let the search for 'perfect' stop you taking the steps that will let you create it in the first place.

25
The Free Range Faststart

O ver the last few chapters we've talked about starting from *who* you are. Now let's change gears a little and talk about starting from *where* you are. Which, in many cases, will be *somewhere around the start.*

The following chapters are 'behind the scenes' approaches to get things going more effectively – especially when starting out with something new (in a crowded space).

We'll cover approaches that are a) more do-able than people realize and b) make a real difference to how well things will work for you, no matter what your 'Style'.

Some topics coming up include:

- going from zero to clients;
- getting status;
- coming across as well as you deserve;
- why you don't have to be an all-rounder; and
- key money topics like selling and 'setting your salary'.

If these topics aren't front of mind right now feel free to zoom straight to Chapter 31. But if you want a peek at these 'under the hood' approaches, read on.

How to do the Free Range Faststart

'You can't stay in your corner of the forest waiting for others to come to you. You have to go to them sometimes.'
WINNIE THE POOH (A A MILNE)

This chapter is a shortcut to zooming your way into traffic and your first pay cheque using one simple system (and a touch of charm). Best of all, if you get this bit right then you can forget your search engine ranking.

I mean it. Using this approach, you can grow a thriving business from scratch without worrying about your Google rank or paying for an ad. What's more, it's something people of every Style can use (in their own way) to get things off the ground faster than most people imagine.

Want to know what it is?

Meet the Free Range Faststart

The Free Range Faststart is three simple steps that let you reach a lot of your people at once.

Before doing the Faststart, you might be feeling like the new stallholder who has landed the smallest and quietest stall at the market. You're in a corner with no one walking by. No matter how nice you make your stall and how great you make those offers it makes no difference: no one knows you're there.

Meanwhile, you're watching another stallholder with a long queue of your ideal customers who are laughing and talking with him. And most of all, buying. How frustrating!

Now, imagine that that same stallholder offers you the chance to join him for a while and get known by those people. You jump at the chance.

You want to be where the traffic is.

But it's not just about the traffic. You quickly discover that the more established stallholder's inclusion of you on his stand is an implicit recommendation: those people in the queue are already smiling at you, saying hello. The ones who ignored you before now trust you because of who you're with.

Yes, they'd love to be on your email list/follow you on the socials; or simply, yes they'd love to chat and hear more. They can't believe they've never heard of you before because your product is just what they were looking for.

No matter you were only around the corner before, they just didn't know to look for you. Now you're on their radar big time. That's what happens with the Free Range Faststart.

Faststart in practice

A few years ago, Rachel Winard was an attorney working a high-stress job in a law firm in New York. She suffered from lupus, a condition that reacts badly to stress, and after years of trying to survive long days (with 4 am starts) she finally quit her job for the sake of her health. As she looked for something to bring in an income, Rachel's friends and family encouraged her to launch her own hand-made soap line using the recipes she had been making herself for years – the result of not being able to find anything on the market that worked for easily irritated lupus skin.

So, she got herself a 'virtual shop' on Etsy.com 'and that's how Soapwalla was born, late one night, in my small apartment kitchen,' Rachel explains. However, once she launched, the burning question was *how will anyone hear about me?* Friends advised her to hire an expensive marketing firm; however, Rachel ignored that advice and decided to do it herself using the Faststart steps below.

It was through this approach that Soapwalla got traffic, gained loyal customers, and ended up being featured as a must-have product in the *New York Times* style magazine (without Rachel ever writing a press release or contacting a journalist).

Here are three steps to do it for yourself:

How to do the Free Range Faststart

Step 1. Identify a list of people or organizations in your field who have the audience you are looking for

When Rachel launched Soapwalla, she reached out to form connections with other established websites where she felt:

> *The people were on the same wavelength as me. I did searches on who I thought would be a good fit and picked out people who had similar goals to me – natural beauty, simple, wholesome.*

Lesson: there is little point casting around trying to reach one individual at a time when someone else already has hundreds or thousands of your perfect customers. Your first step is to identify who those 'audience holders' are.

Step 2. Make contact and build a relationship

Rachel's next step was to get in touch with these website owners:

> *I introduced myself to the people I identified. Sometimes they'd respond and sometimes they wouldn't; I formed friendships with the ones who replied, and it went from there.*

> *For example, there's an eco-friendly products blog I like. I emailed an introduction, explained my product line and shared my story of why I got started and what my ethical principles were behind the production of my products.*

> *The owner responded and I got to know her; we built up an email relationship and I mailed her products to try. She tried something she liked and put a post on her site telling my story in a condensed version. I remember I jumped up and down for five minutes when I read that first review. It was really reaffirming that this was what I was supposed to be doing. Since then I've built up friendships with others like that. That's how I got all my press.*

Lesson: even when you've identified where your perfect customers are, few people are keen to let you leap in and start pitching to the audience they've spent years growing and caring for. Get to know your potential Faststart partners first, and then look at how you can benefit them.

Step 3. Exchange mutual value

What you're looking for is to tap into some of that stream of audience that they have, and the value they get in return might be content for their website or podcast *or* your assistance with or contribution to a project or event.

Rachel offered up her personal story as content for the people she got friendly with. She also offered free samples to her new contacts, which is the physical product version of showing the quality of what you do.

Lesson: don't sound like an advertisement. Be personable, think from the perspective of this other busy person – if they hold the audience you are desperately trying to reach, the biggest payment right now is to get exposed to their people.

For another example of how this process works, in one of my own Faststart partnerships I started by offering a guest post on a website, then I became a regular poster. Soon I got to know the people behind this website, met up in person and through informal conversations realized I could offer assistance both in terms of a) developing some strategies they needed (and which I knew about from my previous career) and b) providing some services that their audience were begging for, but which they didn't have the resource to provide themselves.

The result was that we partnered and launched an event: they provided the people, I provided the service and we both got benefit from something we could not have done by ourselves separately. Plus, I got exposure to a large group of my 'niche', who then joined my tribe (and a bunch became clients!) all from a standing start.

I had no contacts, no status and no reason for this to work other than the fact that I took the Faststart steps: *first understand their needs, offer something of value, then get to know them better (by really listening) and offer something that will work for both of you.*

These three steps can take you from unknown to being seen by tens of thousands of people in your niche, with the bonus of a tacit recommendation from an authority those people already trust. Much smarter than randomly sticking up flyers hoping they get noticed, right?

There are many variations of the three steps (for example in Connie's story, which you'll see in the following chapter, she showcased *them* on her blog first) but it always starts with this:

Attitude alignment: ask the right question

Right now you're in an amazing position. Thanks to social media you can now follow anyone and send them a message (without asking a gatekeeper for permission). Thing is, so can everyone else.

To stand out from the crowd make sure you're asking yourself the right question. The question is not just 'How can that person benefit me?'; the bigger point is 'How can I benefit *them*?'

Look, I know you wouldn't run up to a stranger on the street, grab them by the lapels and shout *let me market to your people!* So let's not do that online. Focus on them, on their needs, and what you can contribute. Remember: there's no rule that you must be offered, well, *anything* in return for your support or time, so only do what you would be willing to do for free anyway. Always consider, *would I want to have coffee with this person if I wasn't going to get anything out of it?*

Choosing your Faststart partners

Here are two different types of Faststart partners:

1. Different from you

A person or organization that covers the broader topic in which you have a niche. For example, a women's personal fitness podcast or offering would be a great place to focus if you offer personal fitness during pregnancy. From their perspective, you add value by coming in with a specialization that will chime with a portion of their niche, but which they haven't yet covered in much detail.

A variation is to go to somewhere with a completely different topic to yours and focus on reaching your niche within that audience. For example, Benny of *Fluent in Three Months* says:

> I don't write on other language blogs. You can guest-post completely out of your niche; just combine the two topics and put a relevant theme on it. On a finance website I did a post on how to learn a foreign language without spending a cent. On Leo Babauta's Zen Habits (*a minimalist and simple living blog*) the post was on the simple way to learn foreign languages. The 20 per cent of readers interested in learning more about what you do will go to your site.[5]

2. Your direct competitors

I prefer to call competitors 'comparables': just because you're similar doesn't mean you have to fight it out. More often than not, there's room for co-promotion, collaboration and many bonding sessions over coffee! *Connecting* rather than competing can lead to the richest and most rewarding relationships.

Faststart with Style

You can use the Faststart to get moving no matter what your Style, so that you aren't sitting around waiting for lady luck to drop by!

Attractors can use this to get things going when they don't have a following (see my example above).

Trusted People can get a boost by focusing on an individual (*or* a platform) that attracts their niche and proving the quality of the relationship (and their work) – like my Trusted Person client Louise, who went from zero to fully booked from two Faststart connections before she had time to even sort a proper website! (Short version: she did some work for two Attractors, who loved her so much they recommended her in their groups and it went from there.)

And **Connectors** are often so at home with this one that some choose to keep using the Faststart well beyond starting out!

Use this as part of your toolkit to get going – and as always, feel free to put your own spin on it.

FREE RANGE PROFILE
Connie's story

'I earned more in one month than I did in three months in my job'

Connie Solera was an art teacher who dreamed of being a 'real artist'. She loved her students and the opportunity to inspire their creativity, yet the admin and bureaucracy that went along with her teaching role left her feeling drained at the end of each day.

On the drive to work – her favourite 30 minutes of the day – Connie would imagine what it would be like to be able to spend her days creating, connecting with other artists and moving around at her own pace in places that inspired her. Of course, this was just a dream. Connie had always been told it was impossible to make a living from art. Art was what you did on the side of a real job.

Then, Connie started up a little blog as a way to connect with other artists. That blog was *Dirty Footprints Studio*:

> *Back then, every Sunday I'd be sitting on the couch wearing my pyjamas, thinking 'I don't want to have to go to work tomorrow'. I had my laptop out and loved working on Dirty Footprints... but I kept thinking 'I have to have health insurance, I have to have the benefits I get as an employee, I just have to work'.*

> *As the sun was setting through the window, I felt like I was watching an egg timer – every Sunday on that couch, how long do I have? How long until Monday, how long until summer break? It was all one big countdown until my spare time when I could live my real life.*

Around this time, Connie also got into art journaling. She decided to share her personal journaling process via YouTube videos. Art journaling was a hot topic. Her videos became popular and sent traffic to Connie's website.

Connie didn't expect this, but once it happened she made the most of it. While still in her job, she created a series called '30 Journals 30 Days', interviewing 30 well-known artists on their own journals. Connie published the 30 interviews as blog posts. At the same time, she was launching her first paid online pro-gramme – 'Art Journal Love Letters' – so, to promote it, she placed a PayPal 'buy' button for the course at the bottom of each of the 30 interviews.

'The 30 artists that I interviewed sent their followers to my website to read their posts,' Connie explains, 'and my numbers grew massively.' (This was her 'Faststart'!) As a result, little newbie Connie sold out the first live round of her online programme (and the ongoing version of the programme ended up selling more than 300 places). 'That made me think, hey, maybe this can work!' But still fears of an unreliable income held Connie back.

That summer, Connie ramped things up a notch. She launched BIG, her fearless painting online adventure, and 'It sold really well. Within one month I'd made more money than I would make in three months as a teacher and I loved every minute of it.'

The first BIG course launched on 4 July.

On 6 July, Connie quit her job and went free range.

Today, Connie runs *Dirty Footprints Studio* full-time – for a while she was selling her art (ending up with 48 commissions in one year) but she now focuses on inspiring and helping people to tap into their own creativity as artists. She paints every day, and her courses are so popular they often sell out before public announcement:

> *I don't know what day it is half the time! It's one amazing big blur. When I stopped looking for something to fall back on that's when I fell right into the thing I was meant to be doing.*

Keep in mind that when she started out, Connie was still working full-time, leaving the house at 7.30 am every day.

> *I was working on Dirty Footprints in every spare moment I could find: writing, videoing and running courses, and of course creating my own art. I was even trying to sneak it in at work. I knew I wanted to make this happen more than anything.*

Connie didn't have hidden advantages or contacts. Everything was built up using her passion, gentle enthusiasm… and a good dose of the Free Range Faststart.

26
Instant status

'It's all in the mind.'

GEORGE HARRISON

Molly heard all this and loved it. She was excited to get going herself, except for one niggling doubt. Molly wasn't sure that anyone would take her seriously. After all, she pointed out, she had never been employed in the field to which she wanted to move. As Molly browsed other people's profiles she grew more and more frustrated that there were dozens of people targeting her niche and all of them had better *status* than she did.

> WTF? This one has delivered seminars on the topic at universities, that one has been featured in the national press, this one has a background at top companies and has a popular podcast!

> 'How can I possibly compete? Why would anyone want to connect with me for the Faststart or hire me when I'm so new and don't have any status?'

Ever felt that way? You're not alone. Fear of having not enough status is a major reason a lot of people never get going. Now here's the part many people don't like to talk about: *Molly was right.*

It's the fault of that dodgy car salesman

We've all been ripped off. No one likes the feeling of realizing they've 'been had'. Sure, you've had more good than bad human interactions, but our brains are wired so that we remember a bad experience more easily than a good one (as John Gottman's studies show, it takes five positive experiences to make up for one negative experience in a relationship).[6]

All it takes is the memory of that time you bought that dodgy car... and bam. Right into the land of fear.

Then there's the fear of making a mistake that is strong enough to hold people back from trusting or connecting with a not-yet-validated newbie.

Here's how status can help.

Status is reassuring

I like the fact that my doctor has a degree certificate on her wall. It's comforting. That certificate is a reassuring sign saying *I know what I'm doing*. Usually you don't read every word on the certificate. You might not even notice it's there. But your subconscious certainly notices and treats this person differently.

When it comes to your situation, the primary job of status is to *extinguish the fear* that may hold back potential clients (or collaborators) from taking you on. The secondary job of status is to *raise your value* so you can charge what you're worth.

Here's how to build that status much faster than most people imagine.

Status hacking 101

When I started out in a new field I was as status-free as anyone else. I went out to change that:

- Within a few weeks (before quitting my job) I had delivered seminars at universities.

- Two months in and I was published on some of the most popular websites for my niche.

- Three months in and I was quoted as an expert in a book, and profiled in national press.

- Six months later, I'd not only got a popular organization in my new field to take me on with an exclusive contract to run classes (ie guaranteed access to my niche) but they offered to pay me for the privilege... even though others were lining up to do it for free. I was also being asked to give talks at events I had previously just watched from afar.

The outcome? I had the confidence and credentials to get the work I wanted at the rates I needed to charge. Again, this wasn't luck, it was down to combining the Faststart with a simple approach to zooming up the status ladder.

The techniques in this chapter are based on a simple concept. Most people think status is an immutable fact, an impenetrable fortress. It is not. Status is simply people's *perceptions* about you.

When you delve into these perceptions, they turn out to take a pretty predictable form: pull apart any 'About' page that works and you'll see the same building-block patterns again and again. Once you understand these predictable building blocks of status, and which status indicators have the biggest impact, then you can skip the years of trial and error and replicate them for yourself.

Three pillars of instant status

These building blocks fall into three categories:

Figure 26.1 Association, publication, quality: the three pillars of status

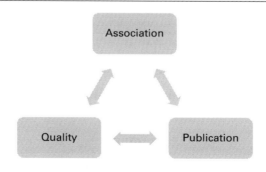

Here's what they mean and how you can create them for yourself:

1. Association

The way we take in the world is informed by associating one thing with another. We see a young guy driving an open-top Porsche and without thinking about it, assume he is well-off. Of course, he might be a struggling student borrowing the car from a friend in order to take her dog to the groomer... but if we were to stop and think of every conceivable explanation for every single thing we see, we would never get past our front door. So our brain makes shortcuts: *that car = rich*. That's how we get through the day.

Your people take in the world in exactly the same way. So, what are they using to make assumptions about you? That's where status by association comes in. Status by association is when you associate yourself with something that already has status in your niche's eyes. That status-giver could be a household-name brand, a prestigious venue, an academic institution, a profession, an award or background, or anything else holding status. Right now your people don't know who you are, and to help them get comfortable enough to want to find out, it helps to give them something familiar and reassuring.

Here are some ways to get status by association in three minutes, three days or three weeks.

Three-minute status-by-association hack

Start by drawing on what you have.

For example, Helen was starting afresh as a hypnotherapist specializing in stress reduction for professionals. She didn't have connections in that field and was afraid she would have to start at the bottom. However, she was coming out of a 10-year career working with some well-known household-name brands. Helen didn't think this was relevant as she'd never worked on 'stress' in these roles, but after we worked together, she quickly saw that there was a link:

> *After a 10-year career working for [Very Big Company, Name You Would Know], and with directors of start-ups, I have witnessed first-hand the impact of stress, and discovered the most effective ways of...*

Can you see how this has more impact than just writing, 'I'm a new hypnotherapist making a career change, hire me!'

I know one seven-figure-earning speaking trainer whose personal brand includes being a former medical doctor. No one imagines that her medical background has any relation to her current work – but it lends immediate credibility.

You don't need a big company, institution or profession linked to your name: another quick win is numbers. How many countries have you been to or worked in? How many kids do you have (if relevant to your business!)? How many books have you read on the topic? Did you attend teachings by any big names you care to mention?

Those are just a few examples. Get creative. You're not 14 years old, so you will have some status, somewhere. Identify that and put it out there to reassure your people.

Three-day status-by-association hack

This option lets you borrow someone else's status.

Find some friends, or friends of friends, who have – or are associated with – status that your niche would recognize. Offer them a freebie.

For example, if you're trying to get going as a coach for creative types, the line 'coached creatives from companies such as Twitter and Snapchat' has more impact than a full page of text. A testimonial from one of these people is even better.

Three-week status-by-association hack

Give a talk at an institution, event or famous venue with status that your target clients will recognize.

Before I quit my job, I made a list of everyone I knew with university connections, and of every institution I could contact myself. Then I contacted a friend of a colleague who worked in a forward-thinking academic institution. I highlighted the parts of my background I knew would interest him. I made the offer to run some seminars there on a specific topic, to get some experience and pass on some free insights to his students. Within a week I was able to edit my 'About' page to say 'Delivered seminars on this topic at a university'.

2. Publication

I remember meeting someone who had recently taken on an image consultant. 'She was expensive,' my new friend explained, 'and I had to save to afford her services, but I wanted to use the best: *she's a published author and has been featured in the press and everything*'.

See what happened there? Status by publication (in a book and magazines) was correlated with being a leader in that field. We think: the magazine 'chose' them, ergo they must be good. Luckily you don't have to wait to be chosen for that to happen. Today, you can pick yourself.

Pick yourself

Today, we're at a point in history where, more than ever, you can pick yourself. Traditionally closed industries such as publishing, television and business are opening up to people who break the rules and make things happen.

Take writing a book. So many people I know who got a non-fiction book deal in the last few years were approached by a publisher as a result of their blog (or in a few cases, a free e-book that was spreading around the internet). This makes sense: with more and more people producing and publishing online, why take a bet on someone who just *claims* they can write? It's also becoming more and more attractive to self-publish.

Or, publish yourself online. A client got a slot writing as an expert for the prestigious *Huffington Post* within a month of starting her business. She identified her niche and status using the techniques in this book, and then building on those stepping stones approached them directly and was accepted.

Prefer live interaction? Get known as the person who runs a regular 'go to' event for people in your niche. Launch your first informal event (share it on Facebook events or Eventbrite if you don't have a website). Your first one might get five people in the pub but keep going and soon you'll be able to say you're running 'this city's only monthly event for over-50s adventure travellers'.

Bottom line: don't wait to be noticed before you start; start so that you get noticed. By deciding to start your thing, and putting it out there, you get good and get known and people come to you: much smarter than waiting to be picked, 'just because'.

Mini case study

I always loved writing about travel and international issues but the idea of being a published travel writer was a bit of a fantasy. I'm a 30-year-old with a regular job, I thought, why would anyone publish *me*?

One day I started a blog. I worked at it for a while, not thinking anyone was reading it, but writing nonetheless. This year my piece on travelling as a single woman in Morocco got picked up by a Lonely Planet website. After that, I took a short evening class in travel writing and then pitched a piece to the *Guardian* newspaper. I suddenly found myself published in the *Guardian*'s Travel section, writing about the top ideas festivals around the world!

It's a revelation that you just do things and then other things happen. I know that sounds obvious but really, it's amazing how much comes from just doing.

Kim Willis

3. Quality

You can usually tell if someone has status by the way they present themselves. Quality is simple: have integrity, deliver great work, and care for your people above all.

As Ms Cupcake says, 'We are fun and flirty but above all a premium brand. I'll throw away a whole tray of cupcakes if the quality is not perfect.' That dedication to quality contributes to her well-earned status.

Quality perception backs up this dedication to quality. That means no random ads cluttering up your website, and using a nice, clear picture of you on your social media profiles and your website (not that blurry one your friend took on a night out once, even if it *is* the best photo of you, ever).

Finally, remember that no one wants to dine in an empty restaurant. Don't do yourself down by hustling desperately for one client... That just tells the world that others don't want what you have to offer, which definitely doesn't suggest high status. In contrast, one newbie I know would leave empty spots rather than hustle for the last dollar. That paid off because she got the reputation of always selling out, of being in demand, and consequently that became a self-perpetuating belief. Soon her courses *were* selling out. That's the power of quality perception.

Above all, do it for real. As Henry Ford said, 'You can't build a reputation on what you say you're going to do.' Every time you take action, hit publish, make that call, you're taking another block to build that reputation, differentiating you from the scores of people who just talk about their ideas.

Bonus: 'Dos and Don'ts of Getting Press'. Download this (short and sensible!) extra page here: http://frh.me/gettingpressdosanddonts

---

27
How to communicate in an unsucky way

'If you can't explain it to a six-year-old, you don't understand it yourself.'

ALBERT EINSTEIN

Something strange happens when some people start describing their business. Within the first sentence, the Confusion Genie lands in their path. The Genie takes out a wand and casts a spell in which simple, tangible ideas become general and meaningless.

For example, take this clear idea:

I declutter your home-office space so you can actually see your desk – and show you quick and simple ways to keep it that way forever.

Versus:

I employ a range of innovative and goal-specific techniques to remove extraneous physical build-up and realign your domestic work environment with your personal and business goals in the short and long term.

Whaaat? (It's OK, I didn't get it either.)

I'm sure you've heard something like that before. This is a leftover of the 1980s style that author Hugh MacLeod calls *Dinosaurspeak*:

Ninety-five per cent of marketing talks to us in Dinosaurspeak. This style of marketing lingo was pretty universal a few years ago, which in Internet time was like the Mesozoic era...

But now, markets have become smarter and faster... language has changed and Dinosaurspeak must face extinction. Talk like a human being, not like one of Stalin's apparatchiks. People are hardwired to respond favourably to that.[7]

The first thing most people do when describing their business 'officially' is to remove their personality and their real thoughts from their communication.

Dinosaurspeak removes the heart of so many potentially great business ideas. That second declutter above, the one who tried to look smart and 'professional', forgot that when you get down to it, their clients really, honestly *want to be able to see their desks and stop feeling so overwhelmed about it all.*

As a result they failed to communicate the service in a way that resonates with the client. Or, in human-speak, *their description sucks.*

Ironically, this attempt to look businesslike removes the very factor that is core to the success of any business – namely, *speaking the words that are in the clients' heads.* I seriously doubt that anyone is waking up in the middle of the night thinking, 'Oh no! I have to sort out that extraneous physical build-up and realign my domestic work environment with my personal and business goals! I hope someone shows up with a range of innovative and goal-specific techniques.'

More likely it is, 'That darn desk is overflowing with papers, I can't find anything and my partner won't stop nagging me about the mess. Gah, too complicated to take on right now!' Listen to what they're thinking and speak to that.

Speak human

As Dan Pallotta wrote in the *Harvard Business Review*, 'When I was younger, if I didn't understand what people were saying, I thought I was stupid. Now I realize that if it's to people's benefit that I understand them, but I don't, then they're the ones who are stupid.'[8]

Using abstract buzzwords in place of meaningful language is not a new phenomenon. George Orwell spoke about it in his 1946 essay 'Politics and the English Language'[9] where he spoke out against what he saw as a 'mixture of vagueness and sheer incompetence' in contemporary writing:

> As soon as certain topics are raised, the concrete melts into the abstract and no one seems able to think of turns of speech that are not hackneyed: prose consists less and less of words chosen for the sake of their meaning, and more of phrases tacked together like the sections of a prefabricated hen-house.

That essay could equally have been written about sucky business-speak today. In an attempt to look professional, meaning gets stripped away. Here's how to do things differently.

First get the words right, then get the word out

A common question asked by people starting a business is, 'How do I get the word out there?' But the best marketing techniques in the world mean nothing *until you have meaningful words to get out there.* There is no point reaching 1,000 people if they don't connect with what you have to say. You'll lose all that investment you put into getting noticed as no one will stick around!

You don't have 20 minutes to describe your business to each person who might be interested. You have a sentence or two in which they'll either get it and love it or nod, smile and go away. So let's make those sentences count.

Practise using clear language even to yourself. The way you speak about your business to yourself is crucial. If you were the confusing declutterer above, it would be very easy to lose sight of who your customers were, what they really wanted and what you were really providing. That's when a previously great idea gets mangled and fails.

So, when describing your business – be it face to face, in your social media bio, or on your first website, ask yourself, 'Is this what I *really* mean?'

Are you choosing words for their meaning, for their imagery and the feelings/ideas they evoke? Or are you choosing them because 'that's just what people in my industry should say'? If so, go back to basics and explain it in a way that a six-year-old would understand, then grow from that. Finally, write all your communications as if you were writing to a particular individual.

That encourages you to speak like you would to a human (not a 'prospect'). You'll know you've got it right when people respond by saying things like:

- 'I'm so relieved, I thought I was the only one who thought that!'
- 'Did you write this for me?'
- 'Are you living in my head?'
- Often followed by 'Do you take cash or card?'

In contrast, use Dinosaurspeak and the usual response is, 'That's nice, I should check you out sometime' (code for 'hmm, I wonder what's on TV tonight?').

Exercise: Four steps to unsucky communication

Be a language detective and listen to the words your people actually use.

If you've ever been in the position those in your niche are in, then try this exercise now (if you have never been in their position, do this exercise after spending time with your niche and actively listening to them talking about your topic):

1 Take a sheet of paper and write out the exact words you said to yourself when you were back in the situation that you're helping them with now. For example, if you're a voice coach

helping new voice-over artists build the skills to get commercial gigs, back when you were that budding voice-over artist, you might have said, 'I really want to get into this but I don't know who to call or whether my voice is even good enough!'

2 Get specific: did you use any particular phrases when you were thinking about this? For example, that voice-over artist might have thought, 'Maybe this is just a pointless dream. It feels like a closed shop where you only get jobs if you're on the inside.' Write yours down.

3 Now go for gold: was there anything you felt or thought that you never dared articulate to anyone else? Something too silly to say out loud? Write that down and circle it, highlight it, stick gold stars on it. I guarantee you're not the only person to have felt or thought that.

4 Once you have identified words that resonate and remind you of how you *really* felt back then, write a paragraph description of what you do, and who you do it for, giving these words a starring role.

Anyone can slap down some Dinosaurspeak. It takes a bit more thought to speak human, but it's a language well worth learning.

28
Why you don't have to be an all-rounder

(you don't have to do it all alone)

'To be yourself in a world that is constantly trying to make you something else is the greatest accomplishment.'

RALPH WALDO EMERSON

As we've been covering these topics, I'm wondering how you feel about doing them in practice. I know when I was starting out I'd hear something, think 'That's a great idea!' and then get bogged down on the implementation. Sometimes this is just because it's a new concept: there's a bit of a learning curve, and then you'll be fine. But in other cases, it's because an approach requires you to do something that doesn't play to your strengths and you know isn't ever going to go smoothly.

As you now know, you can follow the strategies of top business gurus in the world, but if those strategies are out of line with your personality, they'll stall. Why tell yourself you 'must' build your business by going to networking parties five nights a week if you're a solitary type who does better with the written word (and vice versa)? You may get something from those 'out of flow' techniques, but they won't be the main reason you shine (plus, you'll hate it).

The good news is, when you know your personality profile it's much easier to home in on which strategies to follow and easily

29
How to sell without selling your soul

Imagine this: your brand is out there for real. Your website is up and looking mighty fine. You're getting Faststart connections all over the place. *You're smoking hot right now.* Your ideal clients are coming your way and sticking around. *They want more of you.*

You could say the dating game is going well.

In fact, you've met someone special. You're so happy to have found each other – you were starting to believe it would never happen. You don't want to mess up this beautiful relationship... but something is bothering you.

You both know the S-word is on the agenda. That dirty S-word creeps into your mind every time you make eye contact. You are fantasizing about having your first S-word experience with them all the time, in private, but you never raise it in public (well, not without apologizing).

What if you get rejected? What if they slap you down? What if they tell you, 'I thought you were better than that?'

OK. This isn't the 19th century, so let's put it out there. At the end of the day you're going to have to stop just flirting, look them straight in the eye and... *sell.*

Oh yes, I said the S-word! *Sales.*

In our culture we think of sales very much like the Victorians thought about sex, ie pretty often, but never spoken about in polite society.

Thinking that sales just isn't your thing? Trust me, you're not alone. I asked a few free range fledglings their views on sales and here is a selection of the results:

- I just hate selling. I think it's a confidence thing and fear of rejection, but also not wanting to come across as pushy.
- I want to make money but not if it means selling my soul.
- Personally, I hate getting cold calls about products/services I don't want, so I'm really uneasy about doing it myself.
- Sales? *It's just not me.*

You know what feeling uncomfortable with pushy sales means? It means you don't suck. Congratulations.

I honestly don't know *anyone* who loves cold calling and pushing crap onto other people! If I had to do that type of sales I don't think I'd be my own boss at all. However, that's not the only way to do sales.

Instead of selling your soul, try selling *from* your soul. Like this.

The four Es of selling without selling your soul

1. Enthusiasm

Why are you doing this again? Oh yeah, it's because you love it! You are *excited* about working with these people; you believe in the message. You can't wait to get started!

How about communicating *that* rather than trying to 'convince' someone?

If you find your enthusiasm for your subject mysteriously shuts down when you move into 'doing sales', consider how you would describe this were it *someone else's* product you were recommending to a friend who really needed it. Would you want to grab them by the shoulders and say, 'Do it man, do it for you!'? Capture that enthusiasm, that genuine care, and use this at the core of what you communicate.

When you truly believe in and love what you do, it doesn't feel like selling. It's sharing your enthusiasm and passion for what you're offering.

2. Engagement

Forget the idea of sales being like an old-fashioned door-to-door salesman BS-ing their way to a commission. Free Range Humans do it *with love*. To do that, you need to get to know your people, understand them, and above all, focus on helping them. Get in the habit of thinking from their perspective.

On a fresh sheet of paper, identify 5–10 benefits your client will get from taking you up on your offer. I don't mean the obvious features, for example 'a blue box with a ribbon' or 'three osteopathy sessions'. I mean what's the outcome? For example 'knowing they look exactly right for that event (without spending a fortune filling a closet with dresses they will only wear once!)' or 'no more shoulder pain nagging at them day after day'.

Think of your benefits now: will your client get more done (without having to get a personality transplant)? Feel more confident? Have a garden that makes people say *wow*?

(List your benefits in language your people might use when talking about this to a friend. This lets what you talk about connect more quickly with how they think and feel.)

3. Equanimity

Equanimity: self-assurance and groundedness; or, not being pushy and desperate.

If you're coming from a position of thinking you might miss out, that people are out to steal your ideas, and that others in your field are competitors (rather than potential collaborators and friends) then this will come across with a whiff of desperation. When you look desperate, empty restaurant syndrome kicks in and people sidle away. End result: people don't buy what you have to offer.

Bottom line: you have to trust in yourself and your potential before others can trust in you. That's when you stop copying others in your field and start listening to yourself. That's when people buy from you readily.

4. Ethics

Ethics is really simple: treat others as you expect to be treated. That's what being a decent person is about.

That's the way I try to operate, from my personal ethics. That means I don't take people on my higher-end courses if they have credit card debt. On any programme where there are applications I will turn down more people than I take on. I tend to give away more on my courses than people can do in one go, because I'd rather over-deliver than hold back.

That's my version of ethics – some people would go further and think that my version is *too* money-oriented. Others would think my ethics are way too touchy-feely and not money-oriented enough. That's fine. We each come to our own balance based on our own values.

So I'm not going to tell you how to behave. But I will ask you to consider it yourself, get clear on *your* values and *your* benchmark so that you won't be rocked at the last minute by thinking, 'Is this OK? Can I say that?'

Free Range ethics come from the premise that you only sell something that you believe is good. Every moment you hold back is a moment that someone who needs your product, service or ideas is missing out on getting what they need.

When you waver on selling, ask yourself, *am I holding back out of genuine ethics... or are people missing out because of my own insecurities about being too forward?*

That's the big question.

30
Get comfortable with setting your salary

Imagine that you have to come up with an extra $1,000 for an essential payment that has to be made in the next three weeks. Importantly, this is *above and beyond* anything you can pull from your salary or savings.

What would you do?

When you're in a job, your only option is to put it on credit: not exactly a sustainable habit! But it's the option that most employees take. Indeed, when I was back in the career cage, dipping into my overdraft was a regular occurrence towards the end of the month (with the predictable blow-out on payday). Since establishing myself as a free ranger, I haven't got into credit card debt once. I hear similar stories from other free rangers as well.

There are a few reasons for this. The first is that you are simply less likely to throw money around because you know how it was earned.

The second reason is that you can act as your own bank. For example, recently I was riding in a cab with two other free rangers. One of them was visiting from overseas, had fallen into an unfortunate accommodation situation and we were escorting her to a different hotel. As she had already paid for her first hotel for the week, now she had to pay double at the last minute in one of the most expensive cities in the world. Not fun! We made it our about delivering after they buy (rather than feeling like you're doing too much work for too little money).

DO realize there is no intrinsic price point for a certain product, service or period of time. For example, a one-hour coaching session can range in price from $20, $200, $2,000 and I've even heard of a coach who charges five figures. All for a one-hour session.

DON'T set your prices by looking at the competition and trying to undercut them 'just a little'. Competing on price is never a smart strategy if you're a one-person band. You compete for the people who don't want to pay (ie the toughest and most time-consuming customers). And you can get undercut at any moment. *Undercutting works for supermarkets because of their size. You are not a supermarket.* Competing on price alone is a quick route to failure for a solo-preneur.

DO get creative: what else could you add to your offering that doesn't cost you more of your time, but does increase the value for your customer?

DO deliver value. Every time. If in doubt, ask yourself *if the customer gets the results they are looking for from this product/service will they think it was a good deal?* That's what you're shooting for.

DON'T assume people will always look for the cheapest price. There are studies showing that the cheapest wine on a restaurant's wine list is not usually the most popular. Indeed, while I love a great deal, several times I've turned down providers and products for being too cheap. I unconsciously equated low price with low quality, thinking 'There must be something wrong with it at that price'. Trust me, your customers will think the same way.

31
Overcoming information overwhelm

(two 'free range filters' to cut through the noise)

As we roll toward the last parts of the book, let's talk about what happens when you put this book down and turn on your screen.

If you've ever gone to 'just quickly' look something up... then hours later found yourself down an internet rabbit hole thinking, 'so *that's* how pizza slicers got invented!' you'll know this already: *the possibilities for information overwhelm are endless.*

This is especially true when it comes to starting and growing your own thing – everyone from your Great Aunt Maude to that shouty guy in the videos has an opinion on what you should do (and that's even before Top Dog starts weighing in about what your competitors are doing today).

So how do you handle information overload and sift through the noise to know what to take on and what to leave behind?

That's what this chapter is here for. Meet two filters smart free rangers keep in their back pocket to handle any information that comes their way.

Filter 2. Is this right for where I am?

A piece of advice or information can be great for you as a person – but is it right for you *right now*? That's the second question.

At the start, I didn't know anything about web systems – I just knew I needed clients. And income. My first online course orders were taken by people emailing me directly. Payment was done using bank transfers, and then I would email the course materials to a group using 'bcc' from my email address. (I know – so basic. Without a book like this by my side I didn't even know how easy something like PayPal was to set up!)

But the point is this: keeping things simple kept me in the head-space of being 'on the ground', interacting with real people. Instead of getting lost in systems and processes, I spent that time interacting with potential clients (even by email!) and taking real-world action, which gave me important information for fine-tuning my offers and how I communicated them. That stuff, that real stuff, is what matters *more* at that stage than endlessly tweaking a behind-the-scenes process.

So how will your innovative book club service keep up demand, shipping out a book a month to 1,000 members around the world? *Well, is that question right for where you are?* You don't need to worry about shipping 1,000 books just yet. You need to get two paying members, then 20, then 100. By that point you won't be standing at the base of the mountain looking up trying to peer over the top; you'll be at the peak, and able to see your options in a much clearer way.

As a rule of thumb, when you're early on in a project the energy that is 'right for right now' is usually more *hands on*. That means interacting with real people. Here's a behind-the-scenes tip:

Most people you see selling smoothly online today, going from interest to people clicking a 'buy' button with no interaction needed, didn't make their first-ever sales in that hands-off way you see today… they usually did it through conversations (or, at the least, messages!) with their first customers.

In those interactions they got to hear where their customer stalled and decided they didn't really want to buy, they got to clarify something they thought was obvious but that it turns out was not, and so much more. That's what made their offers work, and let them step back.

Remember Amy, who sells products such as waterproof phone cases online while free ranging anywhere? Well she didn't just whack up a website, get overwhelmed for months building funnels and systems... and then wonder where the clients were. No, her first income step was walking into shops and getting orders from the shop owners.

That's 'real life', and my experience with successful free rangers is that the human touch in the early phases means your new thing is getting a good grounding. By contrast, the majority of people get bogged down planning complex web systems they don't need, for a party that hasn't even started.

So when in doubt, think 'hands on' first – and once you get some traction then go hands off, and start thinking about things like 'automating' or 'making things work like clockwork' *if* that's on your mind.

Who I am. *Where* I am. Use those to filter information. You'll be way more free range, you'll breathe more easily and you'll make the most of the information you *do* let in.

Note to perfectionists:

This chapter is here to help you when you have *too much information*. If you have the opposite problem, then go back to the Ladder Game (Chapter 24) and start with the best thing you can see!

Remember: free rangers take action – be that 'Make the most of the resources in the book', 'Get input from people who get it', or 'Run that project and then revise what I learned'. What matters is that you get into motion and use this to refine things as you go. That's how free range careers are created.

32
What to do when you get stuck
(when to give up and when to give in)

This book is mostly about starting, and let's face it, starting is exciting. But what happens when you hit a wall?

Which, by the way, you will. There will come a point – about halfway through your project – when you are tempted to give up. You will tell yourself you made the wrong choice and maybe you just can't do it right now. This is not a bad thing. Sometimes resistance is feedback; perhaps you are trying to do something against your personality and need to change your game so it does fit.

But sometimes, resistance occurs because *that's just what happens to everyone* halfway to the finishing line. When you feel that block you need to know two things: when to give up and when to give in.

When to give up

- When it feels so unnatural you can't bear to do it – *give up*.
- When you feel like your soul is writhing in a cage – *give up*.
- When the idea of actually doing that thing fills you with dread – or boredom – and you'd rather go to sleep – *give up*.

OK, so that idea was not the right one. Change the idea; morph it into something that gets you excited.

However, when you simply lose focus and daydream more than you do the work – give up... for a while. Take a walk, work on something else, sleep. Come back tomorrow. But whatever you do, don't give up on your mission. Find another path to bring it into being.

- If you can't write today, then grab your phone and record it instead.

- If you can't find the words, draw a picture.

- If that isn't happening, change the damn topic and create something that feels right.

Find a way that works, for you, and do that one. Now.

When to give in

There is a difference between *wrong choice* and *fear*. Don't confuse the two. With a wrong choice, apply the above: change the game and try another strategy. With fear (which often hides under the mask of wrong choice) don't give up – instead, give in.

Fear happens, all too often, at the point of momentum. When you move into your flow, *where it feels like you're losing control*, you will think, 'Wait, pull up, this isn't part of the plan. What if it goes wrong? What if it's not the best option? What if they laugh? *Is this allowed?*'

When you feel that way, DO NOT STOP – dive right into the loss of control, dive into the fear.

Do not check Facebook. Do not click away. *Dive in. Headlong rush. Past the comfort zone...*

And hello flow.

You know you hit flow because time flies, and momentum builds and control is out the window. When momentum hits, push through. Stay up later, work that much more intensely, get it out the door bigger and better, do more and be more *and don't let any-one tell you that is not OK*. Ride off the thrill of the buzz of being the full and present you, who shines so brightly when you're doing your thing.

Every creator, every person with a mission, everyone who is doing something that feels so good knows the feeling of flow.

Flow is that moment where something (that is not your left brain) takes over the pen and writes for you.

Flow is where you solve, in 10 minutes, a problem that others have struggled with for days... and afterwards you ask, *how did I know to do that?*

That right there, that's flow. Sexy, seductive flow. And I'm addicted to it like creative crack.

Here's how to score your flow:

1 **Create**. Push. Hard. Don't wait for flow; it comes to those who start. You want to write? Write every damn day. You want to find something that you love to do every day? Get out of that house and do something you love. Anything. It doesn't matter what. What matters is that you moved into its path.

2 **Listen**. To what is and is not working. Listen well and dance with the changes. Learn to identify the moments of flow – they will be the ones where you want to stop because it feels a bit too much – those are the moments to lean in deeper.

3 **Respond**. To what isn't working. Change it up. Stop writing, start talking. Stop talking and start making. Stop thinking about the Reasons Why Not and start listing to the reasons why. Stop thinking by yourself and find another perspective. As they say: *if you do what you've always done you'll get what you've always got.*

4 **Feed your soul**. The best moment comes when you're about to fall asleep after hours embroiled in the tangle of your creation, papers everywhere. You thought you hit your limit and you had to give it a rest. Within minutes your mind stills and the answer comes. Bam. Flow strikes.

5 Float in the ocean, walk in the park, sleep. Do those things that feed your soul. Then, go back to step one and create your heart out.

I spent years fighting flow; I shed tears of frustration thrashing about in my self-made box labelled 'The person I think I should be', hell bent on doing it *just the way it looks in my head.*

Before I met flow, I thought the words 'give in' were for weak people. And then I discovered I was wrong. Giving in is not giving up. It is simply letting go of the handrail and freewheeling your way down that very right path... which to my surprise is down a road labelled 'Get the heck out of your own way'.

Tip

Take your creativity seriously (you get out what you put in)

John Maynard Keynes said that there's nothing more disastrous than a rational policy in an irrational world. He was talking about economics, but the principle applies as much to creativity. Sure, you *should* be able to come up with great ideas and the best solutions by sitting in a white-walled room staring at a screen. But really, if that's not working, then it's not rational to keep pretending it's a good idea.

Take your creativity seriously and put yourself in the best position to think outside the box. For example, in the early days of my business, I was stuck for weeks with no idea how to move forward. I hadn't let myself take a full day off up to that point ('must focus!'). That day, however, I took myself out to morning tea off Piccadilly, went to Hyde Park, took a long walk and ended by the ponds, watching a mother duck and her fledglings doing their free range thing. I came back with more ideas and inspiration than I'd had in a month.

I still take this approach today: one post might start its life while I'm lying on the couch and then get finished when I'm sitting outside. When I create a product I'll ask, 'Where do I need to be to do this justice?' and I'll move, say, to a café or wherever I know I'll get the best results at that moment. You can get into this practice even before quitting your job. Today, segment your home into regions. One for research, one for creativity, one for 'doing the work' and the rest for whatever you choose. If you only have a single room, no problem: decide one corner is for creating and one for planning.

Next, look at your inputs. Are you surrounding yourself with inspiring people who make you feel your dream is possible? It's almost impossible to make a change if you only hear the words of people who don't think it's possible! Even if you don't know any free rangers right now, you can make sure you're reading the right books, browsing free range-friendly websites, immersing yourself in the perspective of those who think like this.

The more you surround yourself with the words and thoughts of people who are doing what you want to do, the more you'll start to believe that this is simple: that 'everyone' does it, and it's not such a big leap after all. We humans tend to believe what's in front of our eyes, and that means if you spend time with a certain type of person you start to believe that their type of life is the norm and your actions reflect that. So average out the income of the six people you spend the most time with and you'll get a figure somewhere near your own income. Average out the self-belief of the people around you and you'll start to understand why your own self-belief set-point is where it is. You get out what you put in, so make sure what you're putting in is benefiting you.

33
Living and working anywhere

(or: creating your own lifestyle)

'Instead of wondering when your next vacation is, maybe you should set up a life you don't need to escape from.'

SETH GODIN

This book opened with a travel story. And I know that while not everyone is into globetrotting, for many people part of the appeal of free ranging is the potential to travel more, or to simply live and work anywhere you choose. Indeed, this was part of my dream when I was back in a job.

Back then, I didn't know anyone who lived the sort of lifestyle I had in mind and I had no idea how to make it happen. However, it turns out that life is much more accessible than I thought. Here's a peek inside.

Hello from Thailand!

As I finished writing the first edition of this book, I was working out of Phuket... in the sunshine of a little hideaway complete with waterfall and palm trees.

This was not a one-off short break before coming back to 'reality'. This was me running my regular life, just in a different place... and with more roosters.

You know the best thing? Unless I'd told you I was in a hammock, you'd never have known. If you were a client, you'd still get my courses, get replies, and I'd still be building and growing my business just the same as if I was sitting two streets from wherever you're reading this right now. There's no difference to my business (the client experience or bottom line) if I'm in London or LA or Luang Prabang.

Is it 'realistic' to run a business from the other side of the world? The naysayers love to say it's a crazy dream that just can't happen. So let's talk about reality for a moment:

- The 'reality' is that so long as I have a good wireless internet connection and my teeny little laptop, I can run my business from anywhere I choose (and so can you).

- The 'reality' is that, while I was in South-East Asia with my business in my backpack, my business earned as much as (and a bit more than) if I was back home.

- The 'reality' is that full-time travel doesn't have to be expensive. In fact, it will probably be cheaper than the life you're living today. It's natural to assume that travel costs are going to be as high as that prized annual vacation from the office. But when you're in one place for a while, you can get great deals on accommodation, you can buy food where locals do and you can end up spending less than if you'd stayed at home.

Sounding more realistic yet? I hope so, because you're not alone. The 'reality' is that more and more cubicle-cage escapees are choosing this lifestyle. This world is filled with people from all walks of life:

Nicole Est (who left 'the job you just don't quit', back in Chapter 6) lives in surf destinations – as well as keeping a home in her native Germany that she rents out when she is away.

Nora Dunn, author of the *Professional Hobo* blog, explains that in her old life, 'I was in a suit, a successful financial planner appearing on TV. Six months later I was walking through chicken s**t and milking goats in Hawaii. I loved it.' Nora has travelled the world in a financially sustainable way for over 10 years, and has no plans to stop.

The Sundance family are a couple with *six* kids. I met them in Lisbon but they live, er, everywhere. Obviously. Last time I checked they were Costa Rica.

As for me, I have travelled both when single and in a couple, with travel buddies and alone, running my business from the UK, Colombia, France, Hong Kong, Cambodia, Laos, Malaysia, and many other places including back to where I grew up – on the east coast of Australia to see friends and family.

Over the last decade I've gone from being bound to one location to being full-time location-independent, and now I do a bit of nesting and travelling. I bought my own place in London the other year and spent over a year creatively renovating it. Recently I've moved across the ocean, to the west coast of the United States, where I'm excited about the cushion potential of the place I'm calling home in LA. With trips elsewhere in between, of course.

This is just a snapshot. There are many more playing out their adventures, their way. Want to join us?

Choose your own adventure

This is how this sort of life looks: *any way you choose.* Some keep a home back in their native country and rent it out while they're on the road. Others don't own a home at all. Some travellers like to hop from destination to destination. Other travellers hunker down for six months or longer and get to know the people and places intimately.

Your free range lifestyle is exactly what you make of it.

Three ways to make any business location-independent

You don't need to teach English overseas, invest in and run a B&B, or win the lottery in order to have the freedom to live and work anywhere. Here are three simple ways to make yourself location-independent:

Choose a naturally portable business

This is one you run online and is quite often a mixture of selling services (consulting, coaching, web design, etc) or virtual products. The main difference is that the way you deliver services is remote rather than face-to-face.

Change a location-dependent business

If your business is of the type that is conventionally tied to one location, simply ask, 'How can I take this idea and make it work virtually?'

For example, when I decided to make my business location-independent, people said it wasn't possible for the sort of work I did. There were a few strands of my businesses that were doing well but which kept me tied to one place. Plus, most of my clients insisted on face-to-face consulting. I was told I simply couldn't make this work virtually.

Of course, as a Free Range Human I just did it anyway. I considered what was most important to me and made changes so I could travel. I dumped the parts of my business that were tying me down (saying *no* to some rather nice income) and consolidated the rest of the work into groups run entirely on the phone and online using the resources outlined in the S100 starter pack in Chapter 13.

I promoted the benefits of being able to join my groups from anywhere in the world. The result was that I ended up with a new, wonderful group of clients from all around the world, who would never have found me or each other had I remained a 'one location only' business. Since then, things have only grown.

Create a time-flexible income (not a remote income)

This is an approach few people consider, but is the reality for plenty of people who are doing this. It's perfect if you want to be part-time in one place and spending part of the year elsewhere.

An example is Karen and Paul. They have travelled for years with a home base in London. Karen is a corporate trainer who runs training days, contracting for a well-established company. So for chunks of the year they are in their place in London and Karen is doing that – but they spend the rest of the year travelling (and expanding their *Global Help Swap* travel blog, which has been featured in the *Guardian* and other places). What I love about this is that they didn't wait to have an 'online business' to make things work – they worked with what they had and created a life full of adventures and a home.

Finally, if you're really scared that your people will be put off by you being 'far away', try it out for a month without telling anyone. You can easily be 'a Chicago-based nutritionist offering telephone consultations'... so what if you happen to be in South America at the time of a call? So long as you're delivering what you promised, at the quality you promised, then no one need notice unless you want them to.

Wait, what about the children?

On my travels I've met plenty of free range families with kids of all ages. I've been blown away by how intelligent and advanced 'free range kids' tend to be, and how giving their kids that experience (often including learning other languages on the way!) is a big motivation for these families' lifestyles.

Jennie Harland-Khan went from living in one place with her family to the French Alps, and after three years there, to Bali. 'We moved to Bali not *despite* the kids but because of them – there's a school there we wanted them to go to, where they would be meeting people from all around the world.'

More and more people are doing this, so there are more resources out there now than ever before, from home schooling support, to schools around the world that welcome kids just like this.

'Where should I go first?'

It's completely up to you! Make sure there's good internet and access to whatever facilities you need. Choose somewhere to stick with for a month at minimum, as that's how long it takes to start to get familiar with a new home.

Some popular destinations for this include Thailand, Argentina (Buenos Aires), Mexico, Portugal, the southern European countryside (Italy, Spain, France), and Bali.

Bonus

What resources do I use to travel and run my business anywhere? See some of my top resources here: http://frh.me/travelresourcebonus

---

Mini case study

At the start my free range dream was to quit the long commute and cubicle, move to my favourite beachside town in England, live in a little home on a hill and cycle between cafés doing work on my own schedule – and I made it happen! I started my own thing, made the shift, and for years I'd think, 'I can't believe I'm living this for real!'

But over the decade things changed. I changed, my personal life changed, my business changed, even my name changed – so I did the exercises again to catch my day-to-day life up to who I'd become. Then

I packed my life into a suitcase, and now live between Spain and Italy in the winter and Eastern Europe and the UK in the summer, running my business from my laptop.

Thinking free range isn't something you just do once – it's a toolkit for approaching problems and changes in your life in smart, fresh ways no matter what. What you create grows with you.

Where will I be in 10 years time? I know I'll be still doing things on my terms, but I don't know exactly what form my life will take. I could continue to grow things as they are, or I could change them – but this time I get to decide.

Now I'm in the driver's seat, rather than the career telling me what to do.

Jenn Hume

'Creating a life'

While travelling is a *visible* part of creating a life, it isn't all there is. For some, 'life on your terms' isn't about travel at all. Whatever it means to you, part of getting from here to there is getting into the mindset of *seeing what you have* in a way you were never taught at school (or in an office, or even in most traditional business environments!). Be it seeing possibilities that others miss, or simply thinking differently about how you use your time, what matters is creating something that really fits you – not building another box for yourself.

Bonus

Want more inspiration and ideas on creating a life – whatever that looks like to you? Join me as I jam with some free rangers you've met in this book! We talk about how they created free range businesses and careers, and what they learned on the way (that might just help you too): http://frh.me/bookjamsession

Mini case study

I was on track to becoming vice-president of a successful company. The only problem was I was dreadfully unhappy about it. Every morning I'd get up and commute from my place in Camden (London) and everything looked grey. My job sucked and I couldn't stand the politics, but I had no idea what to do about it.

On a free range course I was set a six-week challenge to change something about my life. I took it on: I booked a short vacation, got a flight to Australia and lined up networking meetings to find myself a contract over there. Long story short, by the end of the six-week challenge I had resigned, and within months all my worldly possessions and I were on a one-way flight to Sydney.

That's where I'm living now, looking over the blue waters every day. I have run my first triathlon, created a work lifestyle I love, and for the first time I know that I can make anything happen. Oh, and I met Richard Branson on that first flight to Australia but that's another story. That's just the sort of thing that happens when you take on free range challenges!

Dave Brown, Australia[10]

34
How to quit your job

10 steps to freedom

'The ability to invent a desired future is directly dependent upon the willingness to break with the past.'

ROBERT J KRIEGEL

(Already out there doing your thing? Skip this chapter.)

When you're thinking of quitting your job (or moving on from an old business), people might ask, 'How can you throw away everything you've worked for?'

I have a different question for those people: 'How can you throw away your *life*?' That you invested time and money in a direction that no longer suits you is not a reason to go further in that wrong direction. This is your one life. *Don't throw it away.*

I know you've read this far for a reason. Something chimed with you. You're starting to see possibilities, dream big. The worst thing you could do is put this book back on the shelf and think 'nice dream, maybe one day...'

This is it, honey. This, right here, is your chance for something more. You don't have to leap tomorrow but you do have to commit, to yourself, that you are going to make a change. To help you do that, here are 10 steps for taking the ideas in this book and creating your freedom... starting today:

1. Go free range from today

From today, think of yourself as a Free Range Human with one client: your employer. From now on, you work with this 'client' because it is part of your own plans, a source of funding to get where you want to go.

So, get practice at acting like a Free Range Human while in your job. In Chapter 6, I set you a free range action to create a taste of your dream free range life in your regular work day. For example, while in my job, I convinced my boss to let me go to a café for a few hours at a time to work on projects; someone else got their taste of freedom simply by varying their route to work. Did you do that exercise? If not, go and do it now.

Another version is to revise how you allow your current work to eat into your real career (your free range plans). For example, have you let work creep into your life so that you never leave the office anywhere near on time? Is your job leaving you feeling over-whelmed even after you get home in the evening? If so, here's your challenge: this week, say 'no' to a request that is a step too far. Say 'no' politely, but firmly. Don't get upset or defensive, just hold your ground and articulate that, for example, your current workload won't allow you to take on that extra task and still deliver quality. If people are used to you saying 'yes' they'll probably try to convince you to do it anyway, so you may need to repeat that clear 'no' a few times until it sinks in.

One of my friends tried this. Because she was usually such a yes-woman, her boss was amazed the first time she said no, but from that moment, up until the day she left, she was treated with more respect. Every time you do one of these actions, you are building up your free range muscle and reminding yourself that even though you might still be in that job, you're not a career-cage victim anymore.

Those are a few ideas to get you started. Now it's your turn. This week, what can you do to act like a Free Range Human and surround yourself with free range inspiration while still in your current work? Write it here:

_____

_____

_____

Note: Use your discretion. If you have a sensitive work environment and know these actions will put your job at risk too early, adapt them so they work for you.

2. Clarify what you need

Make sure that every day you stay is a day that contributes to your exit, be that in terms of improved finances, clearer ideas, or your free range business built up 'on the side' before you quit. To ensure you are staying for the right reasons, clarify your quitting criteria:

Where do you want to be with your business when you leave your job? *(For instance, I will quit as soon as I have three clients on the books.)*

_____

How can you make sure this happens? *(ie How will you find time to apply the strategies in this book or learn more?)*

_____

Is there anything you need help with before moving forward? Where will you go to find that?

_____

How many months of reserve money would you need in order to feel comfortable leaving your job? (Three months' worth?) Write down the exact figure you want in the bank before you quit:

_____

How long will it take you to build up to that amount? Will you need to do something differently to reach that amount? (Or, do you already have the amount you need?)

Now, if you're going to need to save more to reach that figure, make sure it happens by doing this: log into your bank account and set it up to automatically transfer a set amount to a separate account each payday. This separate bank account is your Free Range Freedom Fund.

Note: it is essential you set this up as an automatic transfer rather than doing it manually. You'll be surprised how quickly your fund will build up when you don't have a chance to spend the money in the first place!

Identify what else you need to sort out before you go (eg US-based readers would include 'health insurance' on this list, and others might include 're-mortgage'):

As you complete each of these milestones, come back here and tick them off. You're on your way!

3. Give yourself an escape clause

The best-laid plans go awry. In my last job, I had been building up my business on the side of a demanding full-time job. I created a perfect escape plan (well, perfect on paper). I'd been running my free range projects (in between 60-hour work weeks), had a brand name and a niche and, even better, I'd finally convinced my boss to let me go part-time! The perfect segue into free range life.

But it never happened. The week before I was set to go part-time, the job finally got all too much and I handed in my resignation there and then. Before I was fully ready. In the middle of a recession too.

In my notice period, I built that website I had been talking about for so long, started on the Instant Status steps and made Faststart connections so that by the time I landed on day one I was already out there.

Finally free, I went down the portfolio career route and added in the strand of consulting in my old field. Getting those consulting gigs smoothed the way for the first few months – and was great practice! Getting out there full-time meant I built up the business much faster as well.

Bottom line: if you know you might suddenly want out ASAP, consider what else you can do to earn money before your dream free-range business is ready. Write your answer here:

_____

4. Set a date

Looking at the above, how long do you think it will take you to reach your leaving goals? Are you willing to wait for that date? If it's too long to wait, go back and revise what you think you need (it is usually more than possible to start with less).

Then, commit. Mark your leaving date in your calendar and write it here:

_____

5. Do it

When that date hits, do it.

Danielle La Porte puts this really well: '[if you want to jump] you've got to set a date and you need to honour the date when you get there.... *no matter what*. Because if you pass that *no matter what* date and you haven't seized it, you start to die. You betray yourself, and that's the worst kind of betrayal.'

6. Get ready for a headrush

You're finally free!

Don't underestimate the rush that comes when you're out of the career cage, away from 'those people' and the daily commute. The liberation is wonderful. You can do anything, be anywhere! You wake up later... no need to rush out the door. You walk to your local park at 2 pm and have coffee with that friend who works odd hours... and all the while no one is checking up on you. It feels deliciously naughty: is this *allowed*?

You get out your computer and work on your business long into the night because you're so excited. There's nowhere to be the next day so you can do what you like! This is wonderful, you can't believe you didn't do it earlier.

And then... fear strikes. Bam.

Welcome to the slump. Every free ranger goes through this. It has nothing to do with how much money you've saved or how well you're doing – and everything to do with the realization that, for the first time ever, you're in charge of your life. You start to wonder if you're crazy for imagining you can do this. At least once you will browse the job ads. Some people call this a reason to quit. I call it your first month.

At least once you'll be tempted by an offer of work that would take you off the path that feels right. You might even take it for a while, and that's fine. But *don't get into a habit of saying 'yes' out of fear*. Every free ranger has a story of the moment they said 'no' to the easy option – and often that was their turning point.

If you want an amazing life you've got to give up the 'good enough' to get the great. That's when things really change.

7. Gather your support crew

When you get started, odds are you won't know many free rangers. When I quit, I had precisely two friends who didn't work regular hours (and neither of them had their own businesses). Now that's turned around and many of my friends can be found roaming cubicle-free in the 9–5.

Get out there and connect with people. Use the ideas in this book to go to those events, contact those people, build up relationships. Above all, realize that you are human, and you will benefit from having people 'on your side'. So get that support crew in place.

8. Learn

'It's probably not a coincidence that most successful self-bossers are also passionate lifelong learners. They know that learning is an investment, not an expense'.

BARBARA WINTER

When I started out I got to know some other people launching in the same field at the same time. Their ventures never really took off, yet mine did. I don't think for one second that I was better than them. But I do remember, time and time again, that I'd make the choice to attend that seminar, join that course, read that blog, and lap up the techniques and learnings that came my way. On each course I would get at least one insight that got me excited, then I'd go home and apply it straight away... and it would quickly pay for itself.

The others, sadly, never came with me. They said they wanted to wait until they were 'more established' to invest in themselves. I suspect that's why they never really got established. When you go free range, you are your business. Investment in yourself and your education is the one thing that will reap rewards over and over.

9. Do

Learning without action won't get you anywhere. When you learn something new don't say, 'Great idea, I should really write that down', say, 'I'm scheduling it into the diary to do ASAP'.

Every day, ask yourself, 'What are the next three things I need to know before I can take the next step?' Learn those three things *and then go do them.*

10. Take the reins

You're in charge now. What do you want to do? It's important you get in the habit of listening to yourself, and stopping to notice those 'oh yeah!' moments. So, you get to choose Step 10.

What three things in this book have made the biggest impact on you? How will you use those insights in your life from now on?

Table 34.1   Free range actions

What stood out for me	What I am going to do about it

Notes

1 Fried, J and Heinemeier Hansson, D (2009) ReWork, Crown Business, New York

2 *What Happened to That Fail: 8 June 2010*, NY Tech Meetup

3 Malik, N (2019) Failed in your fitness goals already? There's a simple fix for that, Bloomberg, 1 February, https://www.bloomberg.com/news/features/2019-02-01/how-to-reach-your-fitness-goals-choose-gym-class-with-community

4 Seth Godin, *Can't Top This* http://sethgodin.typepad.com/seths_blog/2009/11/cant-top-this.html

5 Don't get put off by feeling you have to approach the biggest bloggers like in these examples. Benny had got himself off the ground before making these connections with these people, and he did that by guesting on more accessible blogs – you can do this too.

6 Gottman, J M (1994) *What Predicts Divorce: The relationship between marital processes and marital outcomes*, Lawrence Erlbaum, New York

7 MacLeod, Hugh, 2011, *Evil Plans: Escape the rat race and start doing something you love*, Marshall Cavendish International, Singapore

8 Pallotta, D (2011) I don't understand what anyone is saying anymore, *Harvard Business Review* (Blog Network) 5 December http://blogs.hbr.org/pallotta/2011/12/i-dont-understand-what-anyone.html

9 Orwell, George, *Essays*, Penguin Classics, new edition (2000)

10 Dave since met his partner, Sara Moss, via free range events – which is exactly the sort of unexpected twist these paths take! Sara writes more about her personal journey (and their meeting) in her 2018 book *Go: A Memoir of Wanderlust and Anxiety*.

EPILOGUE: YOU'RE NOT BUILDING A BUSINESS, YOU'RE CREATING A LIFE

'There is no passion to be found playing small – in settling for a life that is less than the one you are capable of living.'

NELSON MANDELA

At the beginning of this book I told you that a few weeks after I left my teens, my Mum died of cancer.

Here is the part I didn't tell you: if you've read even one page of this book then you've heard Mum somewhere in there. She's the real 'free range mum', the secret powerhouse behind this movement.

So, today, I'm stripping back the layers and giving you a full whoosh of Mumness with the five lessons she taught me that form the basis of the free range approach, and that I'd like to leave you with as you start your journey.

1. Be wonderful

Mum was the mum everyone wanted. She loved everyone. Once you walked into the house, she wouldn't let her broken Mauritian-accented English hold her back from letting you know how special you were.

My school friend Claire called her Smiley, because she was:

own unique way of speaking and it was part of her charm and accessibility. You can't be scared of someone who says *loolipoop*.

Free range lesson: embrace your quirks. Trying to be someone else will only make you unhappy. What if you believed that those characteristics that the beige army (or an eight-year-old kid) say are 'too weird' are the very things that deserve to be treasured?

5. You'll win! Of course you will (now it's time for you to believe that)

From when I was a young age, Mum and I would play board games together.

When I was really young she let me win every time, so I grew up with the assumption I could never lose. Mum said that when I got older, she stopped letting me win and started playing me properly.

Thing was, by that time, because I had never had an experience of losing I just kept on winning – my eight-year-old brain didn't understand how someone could possibly be better than me, so I just didn't let that be the case.

This is going to sound odd, and for that reason I don't say it often, but I want to tell you the truth: to this day I *literally don't understand* why you would not think you're good enough.

- Why on earth *should* anyone be better than you?
- Why should someone – not so different to you – be able to create what you can't?
- Tell me again: do you have one good reason why anyone should be more entitled to this than you?

The last question is so confusing to me that my mind explodes at the thought (told you it was a weird one!). Someone once told me that I had a massive sense of entitlement – and I don't think it was meant as a compliment. But I took it as one (well, of course I did, what with a massive sense of entitlement and all).

Want to know why it's a compliment?

Without a sense of entitlement you don't have an inkling of what you deserve. In fact, you probably don't think you deserve anything more than what you have. *And there's little chance you'll go for something you don't believe you deserve.* You may dabble and toy with the idea but if you don't believe – truly believe – that you deserve this, then nothing anyone says will count.

Mum gave me that confidence and belief to create my best life. As I write this book and the words in free range land, that's what I'm trying to give you too.

I spend a lot of time joking and writing sharp pithy messages but I just want to share something with you today: I pour my heart and soul into this work. Sometimes posts flow out in 10 minutes, other times I spend a day creating and throw away 10 different drafts before one hits your inbox. Often I get emails saying 'that part of your message made me cry'. It's OK, I was probably welled up with tears at that line too. *Despite that, I know Mum would have done a better job at this, and I guess I'm just doing my best to do what she would have done for you if she could have.*

As I write to you, it's not just me. It's the care and love I got from Mum coming through, spilling out across the world, and landing in its rightful home: with *you.*

I wish she was here to tell you that you can create your own life. I wish she could show you you're as special as I know you are. You'd have got served up perfect crepes in the process.

While the naysayers are lining up to point out the flaws in your dreams, I know you can do this. I believe in you. And Mum would have too.

Now go out there and make us proud.

Be a Free Range Human and commit to finding another way of doing things.

Be the person who does it differently; be the example you're looking for.

Then, in a year or so when people look at what you have, they'll ask: 'How on Earth did she/he do that? I wish I was as lucky as them.' But you'll know it wasn't luck.

You're not building a business; you're creating a life, and that takes guts.

Go for it, tiger.

Stay in touch! Keep up with the free range tribe, get messages of support and fresh free range ideas straight to your inbox. Get them right here: http://frh.me/stayintheloop

INDEX

NB: page numbers in *italic* indicate figures or tables